CORPORATE
MVPs

CORPORATE
MVPs

MANAGING YOUR COMPANY'S MOST VALUABLE PERFORMERS

MARGARET BUTTERISS • BILL ROITER

John Wiley & Sons Canada, Ltd.

National Library of Canada Cataloguing in Publication

Butteriss, Margaret
    Corporate MVPs : managing your company's most valuable performers / Margaret Butteriss, William Roiter.

Includes index.
ISBN 0-470-83353-X

    1. Employee retention. I. Roiter, William II. Title.

HF5549.5.M63B87 2004   658.3'14   C2003-906733-5

Production Credits
Cover and interior design: Interrobang Graphic Design Inc.
Printer: Tri-Graphic Printing

Printed in Canada
10 9 8 7 6 5 4 3 2

Contents

Acknowledgements

M any people helped us to create this book and we want to acknowledge them all. We particularly have to thank the people we interviewed, who gave generously of their time and truly helped us explore the concept of the MVP in the workplace. The people we interviewed are listed in Appendix A.

We also would like to thank Michael Erkelenz of Fine Line Writers who edited the draft chapters and ensured that the manuscript was submitted on time and in a consistent manner. We are grateful, too, for the help of Cathy Lootsma in Philadelphia, Pennsylvania, and also to Rosalie Prosser of the Alice Darling Secretarial Service in Cambridge, Massachusetts, who diligently transcribed many of the interviews that we conducted.

Our clients were willing to act as sounding boards for our ideas and provide their thoughts and experiences in terms of the Corporate MVP. We specifically want to thank Nancy Folan for her insights and support.

We are also grateful for the support from our families as we researched the material for the book and spent many hours writing. Brian Butteriss provided positive encouragement and

Robin Butteriss gave constructive criticism as the draft chapters began to emerge. Jeremy Butteriss was the one who came up with the title of the Corporate MVP, since he and his brother are avid sports fans. Jeremy was also able to give great insight into what it takes to manage an MVP. Jane Roiter remained good humored and supportive throughout this project, while offering insights from her position in the corporate world. And thanks as well to Brian Roiter for his emergency transcription and editing services during his college break.

We also are grateful to a number of colleagues and friends who introduced us to some of the great people we interviewed and who shared with us their own expertise: David J. Feldman, CLU, ChFC, a financial representative with the Northwestern Mutual Financial Network; Michael W. Hurst, Ed.D., an entrepreneur and psychologist; Stuart Koman, Ph.D., a psychologist and business partner in Executive Performance Group and President of Walden Behavioral Care; Nancy Lague of Bright Horizons; Gerry Nilsson-Weiskott of The Leadership Development Group; Chris Pilkington, Entrepreneur; and Karl Wagner, Ph.D., psychologist at Powell and Wagner Associates. A special thanks goes to Michael L. Michael of the Center for Business and Government at the John F. Kennedy School of Government, Harvard University for helping us to get this project started.

Finally, our thanks go to Karen Milner, the Executive Editor of the Professional & Trade Division of John Wiley & Sons Canada, Ltd., who agreed to publish a third book for us.

CHAPTER 1

卍

Your Most Valuable Performers

You want all the talent that you can get in your business. You know that the more talent you have, the better your edge on the competition. In our work as executive coaches and leadership development consultants, we are often asked to find ways to recruit, develop and retain talented or high-potential employees. Business leaders recognize that one of their most important jobs is to match the right person to the right job, and then to build stable groups populated with these matches. Time and budgets are set to find and develop talent, yet retention of valuable talent is often left to what World War II pilots in a battered aircraft relied on when returning home— "a wing and a prayer." Businesses rely on compensation and potential for advancement, as the wing and the prayer is, as you would expect, still a prayer. Prayer is a valuable activity in your private life but it is no way to run a business.

A Management Need

A few years ago during the height of the boom economy, Tom, a senior executive from one of our client companies, asked us over a working lunch if we could help him address a major concern he had regarding the launch of a new product. The launch required a coordinated effort by many often-contentious departments, each department staffed by a good dollop of talented people driving the product to the launch point. Having just been told that a talented person from marketing had accepted an offer to jump to a new company, he was concerned that her example might create a hole in the dike; others might also choose to skip away with their critical product skills and knowledge, which had taken more than two years of on-the-job experience to create. Without the resources to match outside recruiting offers, Tom knew that he had to do something and do it fast. As all good consultants would do, we told him that, even though he wanted it good, fast and cheap, we could probably deliver only two of his three requests. He immediately chose fast and cheap for now, with good to follow after this product launch was successful. So we got to it:

Authors: About how many talented people do you have in the departments working on the launch?

Tom: Out of about 70 people in the departments, I'd say that about 20 are talented enough to be considered vital right now.

Authors: Okay, think of those 20 talented people. Who are critical right now and in the future?

Tom: About half, maybe 10.

Authors: Great, we don't need you to, but can you name them?

Tom: I know 6 of them well because I work with them everyday and I know 1 by sight. I can never seem to remember his name. Maybe because he is a finance guy and I spend more time with development and marketing types.

Authors: Okay, of the 10 who are most critical right now, who would put the launch in jeopardy if they left?

Tom: Bob and Mike, two of my direct reports. They are almost always one or two steps ahead of me; they keep me sane. Jane in sales; she is magic with our large customers and I know that she is always getting calls from recruiters. And Tina in manufacturing—Bob's counterpart. Bob tells me that she really understands what we are trying to do and that without her he couldn't be sure that product would be shipped when committed. I guess that these four are my *most valuable performers* on this project.

Authors: Okay, let's think about how we can inoculate these four most valuable performers from leaving in the middle of this critical game. This is the "fast and cheap" solution. Later we can talk about how to create "good" ways to keep these MVPs over the long term.

We worked with Tom to develop a plan. Tom kept his 4 MVPs but did lose 3 of his 20 or so talented people. The six-month launch cycle was a success. During our work with Tom we recognized that, while talent development and retention are important, it is *critical* to know your MVPs and actively manage their development and retention in a manner that is specific to their needs.

Over time, as we have talked with senior executive clients such as Tom, we have found that while concerned about the management of their MVP-class employees, managers cannot, typically, point to any specific plan for MVP recruitment, development and retention. They can readily talk about their programs for finding and keeping their "high potential" talent but cannot define a plan for keeping their MVPs. That is what put us on the trail of MVP management best practices, a trail that led to this book.

The Concept of the MVP

Of course, we did not originate the idea of recognizing MVPs. Baseball created the MVP award in 1910 and today most professional sports leagues offer a similar honor.

The MVP award began as a marketing strategy by an automobile manufacturer. Since 1931 the Baseball Writers' Association of America has voted on and presented baseball's MVP award. The formal election process for baseball's MVP is based on thinking that is similar to that used by most business people to identify their MVPs. A clear and organized but *subjective* judgment is made.

As we looked into the idea of Corporate MVPs, we realized that the concept is well known within the business community but is not well defined. We were struck by a comment from Bill Gates of Microsoft: "Take away our twenty most important people, and I tell you we would become an unimportant company."[1] If you run a company, lead a Human Resource function or manage a group with top performers, you know the 80/20 rule: 80 percent of the work is done by 20 percent of the people. The vast majority of this 20 percent is considered the *high talent and high potential pool*. In relation to MVPs, the 80/20 rule should probably be reconceived as the 95/5 rule: that a business's future relies on the 5 percent or less of its very best people. These few key people are responsible for generating the highest revenue; for pulling in the biggest box office; for driving quality; for developing great customer relations; for getting the goods out the door; for creating the new products and services; and for increasing the reputation of the business. We will call these talented people the Corporate MVPs (most valuable performers).

How do you differentiate your MVPs from your high talent pool? Bright Horizons Family Solutions is one of the remarkable businesses and organizations that we interviewed for this book. This business, with more than 15,000 employees internationally, provides child care for the children of parents who work for many of the world's best companies. Mary Ann Tocio, the President, leads the company in partnership with David Lissy, the CEO. During an interview with Mary Ann we asked her how she knew if someone was a "most valuable performer." Mary Ann thought for a moment and responded in her characteristically direct and straightforward manner: "I think about the people who work for me and what would happen if they left the company. I know that they are an MVP if I think that I would die if they left. By necessity, it is a very short list."

---

[1] Quoted in *The 80/20 Individual: How to Accomplish More with Less* by Richard Koch (Doubleday, 2003), 4.

Sports analogies abound in business, often enlightening and enlivening discussions, but we know that there are really no firm and fast rules to identify, to manage or to become a Corporate MVP. Edgar Schein, Professor Emeritus at MIT's Sloan School of Management, cautioned us on an overreliance on sports analogies in the business environment. "The rules for sports are very clear while the rules for business are very unclear." Our challenge is to shed light on best practices for MVP management.

Convert Your Stars into Your MVPs

At a client meeting to coordinate employee performance measurement and compensation, we were looking for ways to ensure that top performers are rewarded for outstanding performance while also building the organization. The manager, new to the job after being a top performer, cautioned, "I don't want to create a star system here." He expressed a core concern of many managers who try to create "fair" incentive plans while trying to keep the best from outstripping the incentives and leaving little for the moderate and poor performers. A senior manager looked a little incredulous and asked, "Why not? I would love to have a department full of stars. If the top performers outperform, then we should want to reward them. We don't want to create a comfortable group of mediocre performers. We want a very happy group of top performers that the others aspire to become. And if the others don't have such aspirations, we'd want them to leave."

Managers have learned over time that "stars" can be disruptive and can create management problems with co-workers. Our MVPs fit the profile of stars in most ways but are different in an important way. Both are excellent performers, but MVPs also improve the people they work with and the organization in which they work. Stars are excellent performers but may discount the people they work with and diminish the organization in which they work.

Organizations do want stars; they just do not want "lone stars" who excel at the expense of others. It is our advice to embrace your top—your star—performers and work with them to help them become well-integrated members of the organization, to become MVPs.

The Central Questions

As you will see, MVPs exist in every type of business. We have polled many of our clients—successful senior management executives, Human Resource (HR) executives and MVPs themselves—and found that the MVP concept resonated strongly with them. They quickly pursued the line of thought and shared their MVP stories. This chapter describes how we identified and worked with these successful hands-on businesspeople, educators and scientists. The rest of the book combines their insights with our best thinking to address three questions central to us and the people we interviewed:

1. How do we recognize and develop MVPs?
2. What does it take for someone to become an MVP?
3. How do we protect our crucial MVP assets?

1. How Do We Recognize and Develop MVPs?

We first had to determine who are and who are not MVPs. At what point does a talented person cross that abstract boundary and become an MVP? While MVP identification is ill defined, we found that all the people that we spoke with could quickly answer this question: "Can you tell me who your valuable people are and why?" We do not recall that it took anyone more than five seconds to say yes and begin telling us about their top 3, 5 or 10 most valuable performers. They quickly integrated the concept of MVPs and easily discussed their great value. We found that once senior executives and HR executives become aware that MVPs exist in a business, they begin to wonder how much value MVPs produce and whether this value should be safeguarded and increased. Chapter 2 will examine the value of the MVP. Since MVPs are "walking assets," an organization cannot lock them up at night. Safeguarding an organization's investment and future value in an MVP requires excellent management skills combined with proactive thinking and basic resource management. It is much easier to manage an MVP well than to stop an MVP from leaving or to replace one.

Chapter 3 will answer the question "What are Corporate MVPs?" We can tell you that MVPs are more, much more, than just excellent performers. They are "performance *plus.*" Chapter 4 looks at how to manage MVPs in detail.

2. What Does It Take for Someone to Become an MVP?

This question can be taken two ways: How can *I* become an MVP?, or, How do I *develop new MVPs*? Both are great questions for people wanting to increase the value of an organization. Chapter 5 explores what it takes for people to transform themselves into one of an organization's most valuable performers. It can also act as a guide to executives who work with high-potential employees who could rise to an MVP level.

3. How Do We Protect Our Crucial MVPs' Assets?

The simple answer is good management. Chapters 6 through 8 expand on this answer. One way to protect MVP assets is to be able to increase your MVP pool through recruitment. Chapter 6 offers ideas on how to create an attractive environment that MVPs will thrive in. It will examine how to identify outside MVPs and how to sign them and integrate them. Chapter 7 will discuss how to recover a difficult or non-performing MVP and what to do when enough is enough. Chapter 8 will speak directly to the important role of HR in attending to and managing MVPs. Chapter 9 will summarize our findings.

The Existing Literature

In preparing to write this book, we searched for other publications that deal with the care and support of business's best of the best. We found many books and articles on recruiting and developing talent and on motivation and leadership. We found little practical advice on how to manage MVPs. We did find some discouragement of the idea of identifying and treating MVPs differently from other talented employees. The concerns were related to creating a special class of employees that could be seen as excluding others; creating an undesirable negotiating position for critical employees; or making critical employees more identifiable by recruiters.

Our interviews have found that our experienced business leaders do not hold these concerns. They understand that keeping an MVP challenged and productive more than makes up for the other concerns, and in most cases invalidates them. Identifying MVPs provides a live example for other employees of what the company values. It also demonstrates to the MVP that he or she is valued, which creates commitment, not extortion. But we will provide more on the value of MVPs later in the book.

The Authors' Background and Thinking that Led to Corporate MVPs

Both Margaret Butteriss and Bill Roiter have more than 25 years of experience as business owners, as executives at publicly traded companies and, most recently, as executive coaches and leadership development and strategy consultants. The authors have extensive experience in a variety of businesses and organizations including advertising, communications, consultation, education, energy, engineering, financial services, food, government, health care, high technology (software and hardware), light and heavy manufacturing, media, pharmaceuticals, publishing, retail, start-ups, transportation, utilities and venture capital.

The broad perspective of the HR and executive issues obtained through our work has pointed to the need for a better understanding of how to work with a business's MVPs. Far too often we have seen the loss of an MVP caused by management missteps and sometimes by no management at all. The very nature of managing MVPs creates uncertainty in the minds of many managers, which in turn produces an uncertain hand at the management tiller. While uncertainty is to be expected given the importance of the asset and the vagaries of human behavior, uncertainty can lead to failure. MVPs can usually tolerate confusion in their work because it creates a challenge for them, but they do not tolerate management uncertainty well. It breeds distrust. Managers who approach MVPs with confidence, shared respect and trust do well.

In our consulting work we have been able to solve problems between business leaders and their MVPs. We have used this *in vivo* experience as the basis for this book. In the book we will offer ideas on how to avoid these critical MVP situations before they occur and how to fix the problems when they do occur.

The Approach

Our approach to writing this book was to consider how to recognize and develop MVPs, to describe how to become an MVP and to discover what companies need to do to manage and protect their MVP assets. In order to gain information on these three areas, we interviewed senior executives, senior HR executives and owners from organizations of different types and sizes. We then asked the senior executives and owners to identify the MVPs in their organizations so that we could interview them to get a personal perspective on the characteristics of MVPs and how they prefer to be managed.

How We Selected the Companies

We wanted to gather data on MVPs from a broad spectrum of industries and from organizations of different sizes. Organizations were selected in four ways. First, we chose companies where we had conducted consulting assignments and that we knew had good development and management practices for their valuable people. Second, we approached organizations identified in business articles and books as having good business and people management practices. Third, we learned of appropriate organizations through referrals. Fourth, during the course of our interviews with senior executives and MVPs, we were given the names of other MVPs and organizations that we should contact.

Using these four approaches, we generated a sample of 24 companies from a variety of industries. The companies included an airline, numerous financial services organizations of varying kinds, professional service firms, advertising agencies, retail establishments and a university. They ranged in size from 10 to 100,000 employees. We also interviewed senior executives from two well-known executive recruitment firms, along with a number of other people who were able to provide us with advice and thoughts on the topic of managing MVPs.

The material for the book is based primarily on the interview data that we obtained. We determined the common themes by analyzing over 1,500 pages of notes taken during interviews of more than 60 people. Appendix A contains the names of the participating companies, a description of each company and of the people interviewed. Here is a listing of 24 of the companies that helped us with this book; the other companies preferred to remain anonymous:

American Distributed Generation	MIT Sloan School of Management
A.T. Kearney Executive Search	Northwestern Mutual Life Insurance Company
Bright Horizons Family Solutions	Novations/J. Howard & Associates
Continental Airlines	NSTAR
FiRE + iCE Restaurant Chain	Phoenix Investments Partners, Ltd.

GeneXP Biosciences	Pioneer Investment Management, Inc.
Honeywell International	Royal Bank of Canada (RBC) Capital Markets
Humphrey Enterprises	Seed Partners, LLC and Growth Point Ventures, LLC
Liberty Mutual Insurance	Shoppers Drug Mart
Limited Brands	Spencer Stuart
Massachusetts Institute of Technology (MIT)	State Street Corporation
Mintz Levin Cohn Ferris Glovsky and Popeo P.C.	State Street Global Advisors (SSgA)

We are very grateful for their assistance and their insights.

The approach we have used is largely discursive and the themes are supported by quotes from the interviewees. Where relevant, we have provided stories and material from our consulting practices to enhance the descriptions of the themes and to provide practical guidance for use in the management of MVPs. We were struck by the high degree of consistency in the data we collected. Irrespective of the size of the organization and the industry category, we found remarkable similarity in the characteristics ascribed to MVPs and in the ways they themselves described wanting to be managed.

CHAPTER 2

卍

Defining the Value of the MVP

A large global organization that we know requires strong people to run its many product lines and business units worldwide. As a result, it places heavy emphasis on developing and promoting what we are calling MVPs. A few years ago a potential MVP was promoted to run one of their key global business units. He came to the position with glowing credentials and seemingly had all the characteristics of an MVP. Indeed, he was often spoken of as the brightest person that the company had ever employed. In his new role, however, his "Achilles' heel" proved to be his people management skills. With his tough leadership style and poor relationship management skills, he developed a notorious reputation that became known throughout the company. Ultimately, he did not reach the potential that people had predicted for him, in spite of the coaching and assistance he was given. After failing at two further global assignments in other businesses, he returned to leading the small business unit where he had started. When this unit was eventually sold, he moved to a new company. Obviously this particular person was not an MVP!

Who are the MVPs that by definition create the most value for the organization? What is it that distinguishes this 5 percent to 10 percent of the workforce from other employees? The answers are not always clear, but over the course of more than 60 interviews, we began to build a picture of the MVP. In this chapter and in the next, we will be discussing how MVPs can be identified—here considering their exceptional performance, what they do and how they do it and in Chapter 3 addressing some of their basic qualities.

MVPs have inclinations and talents that predispose them for one role over another. Some have a greater preponderance of **leadership talent**. These MVPs *create and run the business strategy*. They set the vision and mission of the organization and also set and meet the yearly goals, while motivating others to attain their goals. Others have a greater degree of **explorer talent**. These MVPs *create new opportunities* for the business. They come up with new ideas, make the sales, find new revenues, get the contracts signed. Still others have a greater proportion of **producer talent**. These MVPs *do the production work* for the products or services that generate revenue. They do the work that culminates in sending out the bills. In short, MVPs are not all the same. The truth of that proposition should not blind us, however, to the degree to which MVPs share common talents. In posing the questions of what do MVPs do to create value and how do they do it, we discovered a remarkable level of agreement among our interviewees.

What Do MVPs Do?

The short answer is that MVPs create extraordinary value for the organization by consistently exceeding expectations. MVPs produce tangible and dramatic business results, regularly over-delivering against expectations set for them and for the entire business. They are really able to do what they are hired to do, and to do it extremely well. As Tim Manning of NSTAR says, "We look at all our human resources and try to identify the [people] that we consider to be high performing.... We look for the people who today are really driving and leading performance excellence and who are actually executing against their goals in a way that exceeds what you are expecting them to do."

A more sustained analysis of the question reveals a more nuanced answer. Our research has led us to identify a number of key components of MVP performance. MVPs:

- produce extraordinary results
- constantly strive to make improvements
- attract talent
- succeed anywhere in the organization

Produce Extraordinary Results

MVPs create value for stakeholders by generating the highest revenue; pulling in the biggest box office; driving quality; creating great customer relations; getting the goods out the door; developing the new products and services; and for increasing the reputation of the business. Creating value for the key stakeholders and achieving results involves having great ideas but also realizing them. In other words, the wholly practical ability to execute is an essential characteristic of the MVP. "Good ideas are welcome," Jim Miller, owner of FiRE + iCE restaurants, points out to us, "but clearly implementation is what counts. Someone who thinks about ways to implement ideas practically or even impractically. But getting it done is the unusual talent." Or as Dan Geraci of Phoenix Investment Partners tells us, "there are so many very bright people in business who have no ability to execute, and they spend all of their time talking about the solution and the problem and no time solving the problem or implementing the solution. To me, talent is having the skills necessary to do the job that that person might have, but it's far beyond that. *It's their ability to marshal their skills in a way to produce extraordinary results for the company.*"

Again and again our interviewees spoke about execution in simple, direct terms: the MVP knows how to "get things done." Jerry Bliley, Vice Chairman, Canada, of the global executive recruitment firm Spencer Stuart, says that the "most common trait of these people is that they can get things done.... That's really what makes an MVP as far as I'm concerned. If I had to pick one key characteristic, it's more important to have a person who can get people behind him/her to get things done."

Gordon Bethune, Chairman and CEO of Continental Airlines, explains why early in his career his boss went out of his way to ensure that Bethune stayed with the company. "Because I got things done. The whole world is looking for people who can get things done." Tom Kochan, Professor of Labor Relations at MIT's Sloan School of Business, speaks of advising a young faculty member who asked how to become valuable at MIT. "You've got to be respected for being the best person doing what you do. Then, after that, it's I think just looking for things that need to be done and getting them done. That's again this culture. This place values people who actually get things done." Kevin Wassong, CEO of digital@jwt North America, also explains how he produced results and gave his firm a competitive advantage. "I came in here to start an interactive division, win business and provide a catalyst for changing J. Walter Thompson. I think the reason I am considered an MVP is that I was able to build a team, and we created something that was not even on the radar screen and turned it into a top-ranked digital agency in North America. digital@jwt is a success."

Getting things done can involve slightly different things for different people. Some emphasize hard work and sheer productivity. Mary Ann Tocio, President and COO of Bright Horizons Family Solutions, explains why two of her MVPs produce such strong results. "Both of them are really hard working and they know how to get an end result. They are both detail oriented. They are both pretty fast paced. They both can juggle multiple tasks simultaneously." Dianne Hessan, President and CEO of Communispace, provides a similar description of her "top MVPs." "I think it would be impossible to have two or three people come in and accomplish what they [the MVPs] are accomplishing. These people are hyperproductive and that is what makes them stand out. They have the capacity to do different things; they always, always do great work and they have the capacity to do twice as much as the average human being on a weekly basis."

Others see execution in terms of insight and intellectual discrimination. Bill O'Grady, who led his team to sales increases of 140 percent during his first year as the head of Sales and Distribution at Pioneer Investments, attributes his success to his knowledge of the "key levers of control." "I believe that people think I bring energy and focus, and a clear set of objectives and a relentless pursuit of the same." Gordon Bethune, who orchestrated a dramatic turnaround at Continental Airlines, describes his particular "skill set" thus: "When 10 things go wrong at once, I can show you the one that you have to fix first. You've got to be able to see through all the crap to the one or two things that you need to do first because a million things need to be done. But if you do those two things, most of the others will take care of themselves."

John Marrs, HR Partner for State Street Global Advisors, sees MVPs as "finding opportunity outside the norm." He mentions the example of a colleague who found a way of helping airlines and other companies manage their woefully underfunded pension plans and making them into revenue generators for State Street. Marrs comments, "It's things like that [when you think differently about business opportunities] that make MVPs. I think those folks make the difference between them and talented people who can either create concepts or ideas or take them and make them tangible."

But achieving extraordinary results is not enough by itself to be considered an MVP. Consider the story of a top-performing salesperson in a financial services company. He regularly outperformed his colleagues and brought in enormous revenue to his company. However, his success led him to become arrogant and abusive to his colleagues and he boasted that he would never be fired because of the value he brought to the company. Imagine his surprise when one day his manager did fire him because he could no longer tolerate the disruption and poor morale that he caused his colleagues.

Producing extraordinary results is an absolute prerequisite to being considered an MVP, but is not enough in itself. The additional characteristics that create the true MVP are described below.

Constantly Strive to Make Improvements

The most motivated workers in the world are great to have, but what are they motivated to do? Build their career? Make lots of money? Retire early? MVPs are regular people who want all these things, but we also found that they are motivated to push their company forward. They challenge the way things are done in the organization in order to constantly improve products, processes and people. As one MVP says when asked if he caused problems, "Sure I create problems, I change things, I rattle cages and I wake some people up from that midday sleep that they've been enjoying for years! Yes I do! And I hope I continue to do that." Bob Jeffrey of JWT likens the measures sometimes taken by MVPs to "throwing a grenade into a situation. They're just going to be disruptive." But MVPs aren't simply disruptive for the sake of being disruptive. They are always looking to do things better and to continually improve the job and area in which they work. In Bob Jeffrey's terms, they are disruptive "in a very positive way. They get everybody thinking. They ask the important questions."

The constant push of the MVP for more and for better propels them not only to question the status quo but also to generate the creative ideas that improve the business. They thrive in an environment that encourages questioning, experimenting and tough decisions. MVPs tend toward *serial decision-making*, which is long on action and short on blame. Ned Riley of State Street addresses the value of this for SSgA and for the entire State Street Corporation. "State Street had tactically done many, many things right in taking the strategy of those [internal] businesses that have done exceedingly well and then supplying resources to expand. The [State Street] corporation and SSgA have an understanding that an unsuccessful endeavor should be terminated quickly if the potential doesn't seem to exist. There is no shortage of good ideas to try or of tough decisions to make, and yet individuals are more than willing to make those tough decisions in a very educated and informed way."

Ann Pickens of Bright Horizons Family Solutions not only challenges the status quo but she seeks out challenges to her own thinking. "When I need someone to challenge my thinking, I call on others, in finance, in the legal department and within my own department, whose opinion I respect. I try to have a no-holds-barred discussion where we put everything on the table, and they help me to think through my assumptions."

Some forms of striving for improvement aren't so much confrontational as visionary. Lou de Ocejo of State Street sees the pushing of MVPs as typically oriented towards the future business. "There are a relatively important and small group of people who tend to be the leaders, the visionaries, the risk takers that are willing to think outside the box, who can do the work that needs to be done today and lead where we are going to be five years from now." He continues, "The most valuable performers are not people that are just great at their jobs; they are great at defining the way things are going to be in the future. They are highly influential—this is why things like experience, intellectual horsepower and curiosity need to be big ingredients for me because they are the things that allow people to in fact think outside the box, think abstractly and think ahead."

MVPs sometimes push the envelope even in environments where conformity is valued. Sue Lueger of Northwestern Mutual speaks of such people. "I think that people who are willing to take some risk stand out because this is a culture that is very consensus-driven. It is, in some ways, a big machine and it works really well if all the machine parts work well. Some of the people who are MVPs here were those that at times in their career have stepped away from the crowd and said no, this is the right thing to do, or this is really the direction that we need to take to make things better."

In general, the culture has to be right for the MVP to challenge. As Daniel Behr of Seed Partners and Growth Point Ventures notes, MVPs are "the people that raise their hands, and say excuse me, I don't think this is right, and here's why. It's not just about the blind following of a leader. Of course, you need people running the company who are willing to let others rise to that level of open discussion. I am talking about leadership coming from below the most senior ranks, so the leaders, the designated leaders of the company have to be comfortable with other people taking on leadership, without feeling displaced or threatened." When the ideas of MVPs are accepted, they can be a huge win for the organization in terms of creating additional value and gaining a competitive edge.

Not all leaders, however, welcome the change that is pointed out to them by MVPs. Some may be fearful of change and see the challenge as insolence. This makes it both difficult for MVPs to stay in the role and sometimes to even stay with the organization. Gerry Lupacchino of Novations/J. Howard & Associates talks about an experience at a previous company where he had worked, where his ideas for improvement were rebuffed. "I was the first million-dollar salesperson and I supervised the people who were million-dollar salespeople as well. I found my value to that organization limited only to the financial contributions I'd made to the organization. Any, if not most, of my ideas for continuous improvement in the areas of operations, marketing, and brand positioning were consistently rebuffed by my leader." In spite of his success in the organization he realized that the long-term prospects were not good and began to consider other options. MVPs will often consider leaving an organization where resistance to innovation and change is intense. They wonder how to create competitive advantage for the company if there is little willingness to continuously improve.

Not surprisingly, when in senior positions, MVPs themselves tend to be sympathetic to those who push from below. As John Marrs of State Street Global Advisors observes, "MVPs approach things differently from other senior people. They are not really concerned about being challenged since they've made the tough decisions already themselves. MVPs expect to be challenged and have typically gone through the same discipline and asked the same difficult questions when they get to that table, whereas some of the other folks don't. They just say yes to most of the things that come up, so therefore no one has asked the difficult question where the better manager will challenge. They'll [MVPs will] spend money like it's coming out of their own pocket, and the other ones really don't have a concept of that at all. It's somebody else's money."

Attract Talent

MVPs are a very attractive group, even when you do not know what they look like. There is something about an MVP that draws people in; maybe it is the hope that their talent is contagious. While they may be well known in the industry for their knowledge and ability, they are also often well known in the company for their positive impact on others. Sandy West, the EVP of HR at Limited Brands, describes the attractive nature of MVPs this way: "We have some folks that internally we call 'talent magnets.' Not only are they incredibly strong in what they do, but they attract top talent and they keep top talent. They are very inspirational leaders, and for that reason, we'd shoot ourselves if they said they wanted to leave."

MVPs work to create an environment that talent finds attractive. Roger Brown of Bright Horizons speaks to us about his commitment to fostering talent in his child care service organization. "For the teachers in our organization to be motivated and believe in what they are doing, they need to have center managers and leaders who are committed and motivated. *I've always believed you can't manage people at senior levels in a harsh, aggressive, autocratic way and expect, somewhere along the line, people to miraculously change and start behaving differently.* So whatever it is you want to have happen, where the rubber meets the road, you need to be modeling in every part of the organization. We need a staff accountant who will interact with a center director in a constructive, supportive way. Not beating them up and harassing them and making them feel they are not important. This is needed in every level of the organization. This is a very labor-intensive field. We now employ 15,000 people, so getting the human dimension that is right is essential for us."

In creating such environments, MVPs are typically talent magnets for people within the company. People get to know of them and want to join their team. MVPs also, however, often attract people from the outside. Sandy West cites Robin Burns, Chief Executive Officer of Intimate Beauty Corporation, Victoria's Secret Beauty and aura science, as an example. "She is sought after to speak at everything from FIT [the Fashion Institute of Technology] to all kinds of beauty industry councils and professional organizations. She can usually get us [recruit] anybody we want. When we were building her organization—which is still a pretty new company—all we had to do was say, 'Robin Burns really wants to meet you.' She's known for bringing people along in their careers. She is a developer of people, she has a very charismatic personality and she's visionary."

Robin Burns gives her perspective on why she can act as a talent magnet. "I've always realized that talent begets talent and I learned that very early on in my retail days at Bloomingdale's. I love people and coaching them. Some people have followed me from company to company. I think that I'm fairly good at articulating a vision that they find compelling and that they understand. If it's something that's attractive to them, they want to be a part of it."

At some companies, the pool of talent can reach a critical mass, establishing a reputation for excellence at the company and attracting ever-greater numbers of talented workers into the fold. Ned Riley, Chief Investment Strategist for State Street Global Advisors, describes the company this way: "Its reputation within the industry and within the businesses it serves is so high that people really feel there's a premium in working at State Street, and it can really supercede excessively glamorous financial packages for a lot of individuals. It creates that kind of environment where people enjoy working and do not feel like they are working for a paycheck but rather are working for satisfaction. There's a liability to that; a lot of the competitors look at State Street as the talent pool to tap. That's constantly putting pressure on our resources to keep the superior, excellent people in place."

Succeed Anywhere in the Organization

A physician that we know, Geoff Ginsburg, M.D., Ph.D. at Millennium Pharmaceuticals, possessed strong content expertise in research cardiology and did a great job of managing cardiology programs. As the company grew, its focus grew to include an innovative aspect to medical/pharmaceutical drug discovery and development called "personalized medicine," which holds the promise of delivering the right drug to the right patient at the right time in a patient's health care history. As part of his work, Geoff had developed significant interest in this new and potentially groundbreaking area of research, and he was tapped by his company to further grow the company's personalized medicine initiative.

While stepping out of his area of expertise, Dr. Ginsburg took on the formidable task of creating a centralized function with an independent budget and team, and integrating personalized medicine research and strategy through the organization's research and discovery efforts. He was asking colleagues to give up money, people and initiatives. As would be expected, he met with resistance. Not the "no way, buddy" direct and angry type of resistance, but plenty of the "why should I give up these resources and initiatives to you when what I am doing is working?" type of resistance. His colleagues had their immediate jobs to do and he was trying to implement long-term corporate strategy. We met him when we partnered to support and build his management expertise. He was a quick learner and was successful at implementing this new strategy and eventually having the realistic skeptics fully embrace it.

Although, as we said at the outset, MVPs often have a talent for excelling at one role over another, they nevertheless have a tendency of succeeding anywhere in the organization. This is indeed a rare characteristic since so many seemingly high-performance or high-potential people are not able to adapt to different job requirements, business cultures, leadership styles or geographical locations. As one of our interviewees notes, "I think the notion of being able to succeed wherever you put them is a critical differentiator. They can read the culture well and understand the results that are required of them. They can move around and succeed in numerous roles, such as in a marketing role and then in an operations role and then in a general management role and then running a business role and then doing a turnaround role, etc.; it makes them very valuable. This person is able to deliver the goods time and time again. That is what I would call an MVP." MVPs can work anywhere in one particular organization, and also in many types of organizations. They are strong and they are flexible.

Thus MVPs are able to:

- read the culture well and understand the results required of them

- build relationships
- sell themselves well

MVPs are able to read the culture well and build relationships. Laura Avakian, VP of HR at MIT, tells us that people in all areas of MIT—whether it is on the teaching and research side or on the functional support side—"all adapt to this unique culture. I think it is very hard to be a smart, bright person who is capable but does not know how to work the relationships. I have seen some very, very talented people just not work out here. They don't stay because it is a place that is so fraught with tradition and with getting things done through relationships. Some people can't do that. There is no roadmap to do it."

Mike Campbell, Senior Vice President of Human Resources and Labor Relations for Continental Airlines, expects great technical skills, but the standouts have more. "The value that we put on people skills is one that stands out within our organization. Perhaps valued more than in other organizations, because I think it's assumed that you have the skill set technically in whatever area you're in, whether it be technology or flight operations or whatever the area may be. So, I think the technical skill level is almost a given and those who stand out are those who have the people skills, the working together part of the equation." Continental builds teams the way artisans build watches—each piece is critical.

Knowing how to gain acceptance is often a crucial requirement. We know of numerous organizations with cultures that "are out to get the MVP." Once people are successful in a number of places and produce outstanding results, others may feel jealous or threatened enough to take potshots at them and try and pick them off. This occurs most frequently in organizations where negativity and devaluing is consistently the prevailing culture. MVPs succeed in such environments by displaying confidence and "presence." This is likely to come from a very subtle "selling of oneself" to other people at all levels and places in the organization. MVPs do not expect to be accepted and respected; they find ways to become accepted and respected.

Mark Howes of Honeywell notes that the organization has to be one that supports the success of the MVP. "For the MVPs to succeed it's very important that the rest of the entity that they are a part of is relatively healthy. If it's a sick place then you get a higher probability that MVPs are going to be perceived negatively and even create more problems."

How Do MVPs Create Value?

Having considered what MVPs do, we will now turn to how MVPs create value. Our interviews strongly indicate that the MVPs achieve because they:

- build their jobs to get results
- are team players
- create the culture for team success
- are skilled at developing others

Build Their Jobs to Get Results

Intellectually, MVPs are nimble. They may use job descriptions as guides, but ultimately they rely on business needs, on the imperative to create value, to define their role. As Helen Sayles of Liberty Mutual describes them, "Corporate MVPs are those people who, when they are in a role, change the role. They make it something different. They don't just do the job; they take it to the next level. They are consistently on the lookout for improvement, positive change, how can we do things better, how can we do things differently. They really change the nature of the role." The MVP does not depend on hierarchy, authority or commands. He or she achieves stellar results by bringing flexibility to the task.

In many instances, MVP results keep improving because the MVP and the job develop in tandem. John Humphrey, formerly of Forum, speaks of the MVPs he has seen. "At companies I have been part of or consulted with, I have seen people go into a position and make that position theirs. Talented people mold the position. The position grows, they grow. Good people with access to resources are attracted to their projects. They make it into something. The more that happens, the more indispensable they become. They create a tailor-made suit." John Hatsopoulos, formerly of Thermo Electron, comments similarly when discussing how MVPs at the company developed their jobs. "I like the idea of development. Some of our most valuable people were built that way. They liked to develop. They knew that they could develop and run their own companies. That's why we ended up with 24 publicly traded companies."

Gerry Lupacchino, the VP of Sales at Novations/J. Howard & Associates, describes the culture of flexibility at his company. "Our job definition boundaries or our parameters are blurred. We step into each other's areas all the time. Not redundancy, but continuous support. I don't know that it's expected, but it's comforting. We're all sort of covering each other's backs. We're all supporting each other. Pretty much everyone is willing to step up. And those who aren't don't last over time, because they're just not comfortable taking on some responsibility for other people's successes as well as their own. We all help each other do our jobs in the best way possible."

Taking on a job and then modifying it to support a vision of the current and future market needs takes a special type of person. Change requires new thinking and the willingness to take on risk. Most people prefer not to change and can become downright resistant to it. This is true even if the current approaches no longer work. MVPs are not usually assigned jobs in well-functioning areas that require a caretaking manager. They seek out, and they are given, challenging assignments that require exploration, problem solving, improving and inventing. One of the greatest values of an MVP is his or her ability to identify, confront and overcome the business challenges that most employees cannot even envision.

Are Team Players

Building a job to get results, as Gerry Lupacchino notes, can enhance teamwork among key players. It should be no surprise, then, that **the key trait of MVPs noted by virtually everyone we interviewed is that MVPs are team players**. Team players differ greatly from those people who are more concerned about how their achievement of goals and results will advance their career and make them look good. This concern is "all about me." In contrast, the perspective of the team-oriented MVP is that it is "all about US."

Many of those we interviewed see little difference between the role of MVPs in business and the role of MVPs in sports. In fact, during our conversations, the sports analogy was often front and center. Tim Manning of NSTAR, for example, points out that as in sports, MVPs are necessarily team players. "If you look at the MVPs in basketball and football, they are folks that have high levels of individual skills but are able to find ways to really excel as a member of a team, and play certain roles. I think it's similar in business, not only from the individual contributor but also from a leadership standpoint."

MVPs do not value teams because it is the correct way to do things; teams are valued because they produce greater value than the MVP can produce alone. As part of their contribution to the team, MVPs harness the greatness of others. A colleague of ours notes, "I do make the assumption that MVPs know how to harness the greatness of the people who are in it with them. Think about a sports team—while the MVP often scores the most points or makes the critical touchdown, it is really all about the players who make the rest of the team better and help the rest of the team win." Most basketball players who played with Michael Jordan had the best seasons of their careers when they played with him. However, when there were two seconds left on the clock and the team needed another basket to win, it was Jordan who took the shot.

Virginia Murray of A.T. Kearney Executive Search notes, "I think MVPs make everybody look good, not just themselves. People often think of an MVP as the hotshot guy that's running around and putting the puck in by himself, but it's the whole team of MVPs that really makes the difference."

Create the Culture for Team Success

Some organizations consciously create a culture of teamwork that aims to ensure that all the people act as team members.

They truly believe that teamwork is the key to business success. The Chairman and CEO of Continental Airlines, Gordon Bethune, has created such a culture and gives credit to the team around him for turning this airline around. "To work here and be a top manager, you've got to be the absolute best at what you do and you have to be a team player. We have no prima donnas here who say, 'You can't live without me,' because you can... nobody is irreplaceable." Ned Walker, Bethune's colleague at Continental, concurs. "I think the one thing that Gordon has instilled in all of us is a sense of teamwork. It's funny, you get outside and people say, "Gordon, you're doing a great job." Gordon always turns around and gives the credit to the frontline employee out there, because that's generally who the customer sees. But also to the people in reservations whom the customer may not see, to the mechanics who ensure your plane is working, and to the people who are doing payroll, because your plane may take off but the guy who fixed it needs to get paid."

Walker continues, "Gordon gives the analogy of the football team that's on the field. They don't just put the backfield in the huddle—they put everybody in the huddle. And that's what we do here. We are a team, and when we win we'll win together. Our employees know the challenges that this airline is facing and this industry is facing because they're in the huddle. They get to hear what the game plan is."

Tim Harbert, Chairman and CEO of SSgA, talks about who he values and why. "What I look for as the most valuable performer are individuals who are excellent intellectually in their work, and also in their personality. I look for characteristics that point to open communication, transparency, integrity, decision-making ability, consensus building. I like a player-coach, in other words; they can do the job and they can also coach people, supervise them, mentor them in jobs. They have often come up through the ranks, succeeding as a member of the team. They don't carry an attitude with them...'I have X years' experience, so this task that needs doing is too lowly for me.' They expect to work as a team and to do what is required."

Ned Riley of SSgA also talks about how teamwork has helped move the business forward. "We do focus on a team concept. We do focus on achieving results through cooperation. A lot of the silos have come down or have never existed that strongly in the corporation because people have shared in the success and because equity has been an important component of the incentive programs to succeed. I really believe that people understand the need for growth and they know the means of achieving that growth and the things they can do to leverage relationships and clients in such a way to expand the number of products per client."

Roger Brown of Bright Horizons mentions that each different type of business may need a different culture to succeed. He has consciously created a team environment that has led his business to be successful. "I think different businesses need different things. An investment style business may need fund managers who are clear stars and are treated like stars. In other organizations like ours, we try to have a culture in which we see everybody as having a vital and crucial role. We try to avoid a star culture. We try to help everybody figure out how they can contribute their maximum effort."

Ian Hendry of RBC Capital Markets makes an interesting point about the need for MVPs to be adaptive, both as team players and individual players at the same time. The best corporate finance professionals, for example, have to perform a difficult juggling act, but this is a hallmark of the true MVPs in the business. "Teamwork is key for us as we deliver various forms of human expertise into a particular client situation. If the primary customer contact is the investment banker, their ability to assemble specialized knowledge from the credit group and expertise from the derivatives team and other bright minds, and for them to work in harmony to solve a unique client need is a key differentiator of success."

Are Skilled at Developing Others

MVPs have a way of developing co-workers even without intending to. They set the example. They are the achievers others seek to model themselves after. On the other hand, MVPs typically take a proactive approach to developing the capacities of those around them. They have a keen interest in creating a strong working team.

Developing others may be as simple as setting an example or inspiring enthusiasm. Osbert Hood of Pioneer Investments tells us of MVPs he knows who have "that way of making people around them feel important and feel that the job at hand is important. I've also been around people who do the complete opposite, just breathe poor morale, so it is easy to spot your MVPs because they are the former and not the latter." For Daniel Behr, the workers "that are really good, the most valuable ones, are the ones that infect the business with their enthusiasm, creativity, or action orientation, whatever it is. You do, in fact, want the people who have a particular expertise to also ideally have the ability to infect—and infect is really the word—others with their ideas and their enthusiasm. So somehow the most valuable players to me are the people that are talented at what they have to do but also are able to earn the respect and have others want to follow." Mark Howes, VP of Mechanical Systems and Accessories at Honeywell, sees what differentiates MVPs from other talented employees as "the effect they have on other people, meaning they are able to get things done. People rally to them, people are willing to follow and be led by them."

MVPs, however, do not normally lead by example alone. Their role in developing others is deliberate and active. Tim Manning of NSTAR says that the true MVP *wants* to develop others. "It's really the ability to create opportunities for improvement in individuals by sharing their own experiences with others, which provides for additional learning on the part of people with whom they engage." Roger Brown, Executive Chairman of Bright Horizons, describes one of his MVPs as "a master of seeing that to grow the business you have to constantly break the mold and reorganize and think about who is going to do these new set of tasks. She's a genius at knowing which person would be interested in going to London for a year to do this specific assignment in order to develop both themselves and the business. She is a godlike figure in the company."

According to Keith Brown, VP of Operations at FiRE + iCE, developing others is "part of the operation at FiRE + iCE restaurants. Three of our very good managers are great at developing the assistant managers in terms of the operation. They're very good at holding people accountable; they're very good at getting the most out of them and identifying what people's weaknesses are, and accentuating their strengths."

Checklist to Determine Who Is an MVP

Here is a checklist to help determine who is an MVP in terms of what they do and how they do it. It is followed by a checklist that may help define who is a high performer, but not necessarily an MVP.

✓ The MVP produces extraordinary results for the company—this is an absolute prerequisite for someone to even be considered an MVP.

✓ The MVP constantly tries to improve products, processes and people and to add tremendous value to the company.

✓ The MVP attracts other talented people to the organization because of the reputation they have for achieving results and for developing people.

✓ The MVP will succeed anywhere in the organization because they are able to work with different styles of leadership and in different cultures and geographical locations. They also usually succeed in many different companies.

✓ The MVP builds their job to get results and will change their role for the better so that they can achieve more for the company. The MVP is a team player and recognizes that a team can produce better results than any individual.

✓ The MVP is concerned about the success of the team rather than their own personal success. They are never prima donnas.

✓ The MVP is good at developing other people and bringing out the best in them. They also act as role models for others in the organization because of the results they achieve and the way they achieve them.

Checklist to Determine Who Is NOT an MVP

People who are not MVPs can also produce extraordinary results, but are not considered a true MVP for the following reasons:

✓ They usually try to keep things the way they are and are not interested in making improvements for the good of the organization. They will make changes that benefit their own career advancement and personal requirements.

✓ They are unlikely to attract talented people to work with them since they discount the people they work with, and others feel they may not learn anything from them.

✓ They may succeed in certain parts of the organization but will not succeed in others. They are not respected and are unlikely to succeed under multiple styles of leadership.

✓ They do not change their roles for the better.

✓ They are not team players since their prime focus is on "ME."

✓ They are not good at or interested in developing others.

CHAPTER 3

卍

Who Are Corporate MVPs? How Do You Define Them?

In the last chapter we considered the value the MVP brings to organizations in terms of producing extraordinary results and the way that they achieved them. We will now look at the common traits and basic qualities of the MVPs that help them to achieve these extraordinary results for their organizations.

Some common traits of the MVP:

- MVPs are motivated by intrinsic passion.
- MVPs always want to succeed and do not like to fail.
- MVPs show moral courage.
- MVPs are committed to the values and vision of the company.
- MVPs enhance the company's reputation.
- MVPs earn the respect of colleagues.

MVPs Are Motivated by Intrinsic Passion

Calculated self-interest is often a powerful motivational force in the business world and in life generally. Yet for MVPs, self-interest usually takes second place to an overriding passion to create value for the organization. On this score, our findings are consistent with the observations of Daniel Goleman in his *Harvard Business Review* article on emotional intelligence: "If there is one trait that virtually all effective leaders have, it is **motivation**. They are driven to achieve beyond expectations—their own and everyone else's. The key word here is *achieve*. Plenty of people are motivated by external factors such as a big salary or the status that comes from having an impressive title or being part of a prestigious company. By contrast, those with leadership potential are motivated by a deeply embedded desire to achieve for the sake of achievement. The first sign is a passion for the work itself—such people seek out creative challenges, love to learn, and take great pride in a job well done. They also display an unflagging energy to do things better. People with such energy often seem restless with the status quo. They are persistent with their questions about why things are done one way rather than another; they are eager to explore new approaches to their work." MVPs *need* to understand the "why" of a plan, not just the who, what, where and how. They incorporate this understanding into their thinking to use when obstacles are encountered and when flexible and creative thinking is of value. This need to understand is fueled by their passion for their work.

A number of the people we interviewed talk about **passion** directly. Ed Schein, Professor Emeritus of the Sloan School of Business at MIT, tells us that MVPs will produce results and exceed expectations whether or not they get recognition precisely because they are self-driven and motivated. Osbert Hood of Pioneer Investments speaks of doing what he does because he really enjoys it. "Every year I try to contribute something that's new, measurable, and really value-added and makes a difference." Gerry Lupacchino of Novations/J. Howard & Associates describes his passion this way: "What keeps me excited is that the work we do seems to change with every client—we meet the client where they are, and help move them to the next level, wherever that might be. Our internal technology helps me to be more productive, so what would typically be a distraction isn't. The key factor that motivates me to work as hard as I do is the congruence I have with the work Novations/J. Howard does and the direction it is taking. I am lucky." Audra Bohannon, also of Novations/J. Howard & Associates, identifies her passion as representing her very value to the firm. "I think my value is that I am passionate about what I do. I have a commitment to the development of people. There was a fire in me that always wanted to be able to develop people. That's why when this opportunity to join Novations J. Howard & Associates as a trainer came up, it just fit so well and so…it's the passion."

What MVPs are passionate about is creating value. They are forever raising the performance bar, and they like to keep score and need a scorecard to do this. Once they have achieved something, they want to do it again, but do it much better next time. True MVPs will not get discouraged when the score or results are against them, rather they will stay motivated and optimistic. According to Dan Geraci, President and CEO of Phoenix Investments Partners, Ltd., "MVPs have to be given goals and targets to achieve that are measurable, e.g., sales goals, project completion dates. This enables them to keep raising the bar with themselves and others. They also expect to be given more and more challenging results to achieve and they refuse to fail." Bill O'Grady of Pioneer Investments describes himself as a person with unwavering commitment and focus to achieving results. "Once I'm clear on what the objective is, I'm relentless in its pursuit. I also believe that speed is important, so therefore a sense of urgency is something that I have personally."

MVPs Always Want to Succeed and Do Not Like to Fail

If intrinsic passion is one motivating force of the MVP, another is their drive to succeed. They take on a challenge with the expectation that they will succeed and, as importantly, with the willingness to do what it takes to succeed. They do not take success for granted and are aware that failure is possible.

They watch for failure and use its possibility as a motivator to keep working.

MVPs typically have a track record of success that others may envy. MVPs appreciate their previous successes but do not believe that the past will guarantee their future. They rely on brains and hard work to master the next challenge. Their expectation of success, combined with their pragmatic view of what it takes to succeed, pushes them to stay flexible and to employ critical thinking throughout their work. They see entitlement, assumption, and the shirking of responsibility as the traps that ensnare failures. Their simple distaste of failure keeps them alert and on guard. Some have described this as fearing failure.

Sally Krawcheck, CEO of Smith Barney, and Anne Mulcahey, CEO of Xerox, have both been the subject of *Fortune* articles addressing this motive. Fear drives Krawcheck to achieve results for the company and for herself. Her childhood experience as a social outsider "created an abject fear of failure for which [she is] grateful now but that was awful as a kid."[1] Before assuming the reins at Xerox, Mulcahey was considered smart and energetic but was thought not to have the track record of a potential CEO. Today, however, she is considered an MVP by her board and her employees. Like Krawcheck, Mulcahey confesses that her success has been motivated more by fear of failure than ambition.[2]

Ned Riley, the Chief Investment Strategist of State Street Global Advisors, talks in very positive terms of avoiding failure. "Some of the most successful people in the world are the most insecure with their positions. That insecurity is an asset, not a liability. The insecurity drives you harder. Fear of failure makes you focus a lot more. The insecurity clearly is a motivator. If people become too complacent, too satisfied, it means they have stopped growing and the job then becomes a job and not something that can be enjoyable."

---

[1] David Rynecki, "Can Sally Save Citibank," *Fortune*, June 9, 2003, 78.

[3] From an article on Anne Mulcahey, CEO of Xerox. "The Accidental CEO," *Fortune*, June 23, 2003, 62.

Ed Evangelista is an Executive Creative Director at JWT in New York and, as his position would indicate, is a major creative force at the agency. We asked Ed if he knew that he was considered an MVP at JWT. He tells us that "The problem is, in *my* mind, I don't think I'm that good. You know, I'm always worried that I'm not good enough. And I think that's what sort of drives me. I don't know what *the* talent is. Maybe it's because I have an entrepreneurial spirit.... I mean I left this business for three years at one point, and I opened a construction company." This point is also echoed by one of our clients who tells us that the most valuable members of her senior team also want to be successful, not so much from insecurity, but because of their need to improve the organization and themselves.

MVPs Are Prepared to Show Moral Courage

Many employees are reluctant to poke their heads out of their narrowly defined job. They never explore new ideas, never get to the point of moving into senior management because they don't want to be held accountable for anything more than the minimum. MVPs, by contrast, aren't afraid to make tough decisions and take responsibility for the consequences. They are prepared to show moral courage in the face of a challenge. As Mike Hyter, President and CEO of Novations/J. Howard & Associates tells us, "I find that a lot of people tend to shy away when you really want to create some sense of accountability. But the MVPs are very willing to step into the light, get close to the fire, deal with the issues, and are willing to be held accountable, whether it goes well or it goes wrong; and they stand with the people that have been working with them."

Sometimes a tough decision may consist of nothing more than saying no. Many people think no yet say, "Okay, let's talk next week," "Run it by Charlie," or "Great idea, let's put it in next year's budget." "No" is a tough word to say for some people. John Marrs at SSgA has seen managers seek out the "easy yes" senior managers and avoid the tough-minded "no is an option" senior managers. "When there are tough/big decisions to be made, what will happen is a manager will know who at the top is an easier play than the others and will actually avoid the guys who will ask the difficult questions to try to get some momentum behind the idea so that he or she doesn't get the no." These managers think they are doing the smart thing by looking at the organization and deciding which path will most likely get them what they want. MVPs won't shy away from saying no, nor will they avoid risking a no by hiding from a superior's critical scrutiny.

In general, MVPs are not afraid of criticism. Tom Kochan of MIT Sloan School of Management tells us of how the "best people" at MIT respond. "We've had some very vigorous debates in some of the things I've been involved with and I have seen that we are willing to be critical of people in higher positions of authority and power, and they are willing, even eager, to engage in the give and take. At MIT they are willing to put their ideas out there, and they are willing to answer and ask the hard questions."

For John Humphrey, founder and former Chairman of Forum, being an MVP means being willing to risk looking foolish. "The fear in business," says John, "is not that you're going to lose money in a transaction; *the fear in business is that you're going to make a fool of yourself.* That's what people worry about." Humphrey himself showed his willingness to risk appearing foolish during the annual Forum Follies, a yearly team-building experience in which participants sing, dance or perform satiric skits in front of their colleagues. One year, without prompting, Humphrey volunteered to compose and sing his own song while dressed in a pirate's costume. Since he hadn't sung before an audience since the fifth grade, his chance of making a fool of himself was strong, but he persisted. "This is me in public doing something off my area of competence. This is me pushing myself. The point was that you could take some personal risk. I bet if you talked to the Forum alumni none of them would remember anything about that evening. But if you ask them about John's willingness to take personal risks, they would say, 'Oh yes. He takes big risks when investing in us and he has demonstrated it over time.'"

Are people more afraid of making fools of themselves than they are at not succeeding? For some people, responsibility is similar to standing alone on a stage and singing for the first time since the fifth grade.

Marc Capra of J. Walter Thompson looks for people who take responsibility for their own future. "I think that my key consideration regarding MVPs is that they take their destiny into their own hands. They are not waiting for the organization to give them a direction, but they are really providing the direction for the organization. And I think that they can provide that direction for an organization at any level. They can take that destiny in their own hands and move it forward, and move the organization forward."

Being responsible does not necessarily mean being alone with a burden. MVPs are people who can be counted on to share risks with their colleagues. When a senior executive we know in the financial services industry, first faced the possibility of combat as a young officer in the U.S. Army, "a very large first sergeant" said to him, "Sir, you already know which people around here you trust and there aren't many you can trust with your life. Stay close to me." This executive's experiences with MVPs in the workplace have been like his experience with his sergeant. "It's been the same thing with MVPs. Who are the people that you want on your right and on your left? There aren't many of them that you can trust with your life, because there are those that when it gets a little bit tough will duck when you really need somebody out there shooting back." MVPs stand up for colleagues when it counts.

Keith Brown of FiRE + iCE learns who his best people are when things go wrong. "The good players or the critical people are the people that can manage when things aren't so right. When things go right it's easy to be a good player. But when things go wrong, and things get gray, I think the people that are the most valuable are the people who can manage those areas. When things just get screwed up and you can come up smelling like a rose, those are the good people for me. Those are the people who can think on their feet and can implement the fix."

MVPs Are Committed to the Vision and Values of the Company

MVPs tend to be independent thinkers willing to raise questions and even objections when circumstances warrant. Yet they also tend to share the vision and values of the company. As one CEO tells us, "I think it's sharing the common vision that is one of the ways that I recognize an MVP. They tend to share whatever vision and goals we have set up as a group or team. Not too many people know how to do this." With their commitment to the direction of the company, MVPs have an impact far beyond the scope of their immediate responsibilities. Once these players are on the "team," a business can be built around them. They do not take committing to the team lightly; if they do not agree with something, they will say so and will work on it until they can agree.

As in sports, MVPs are a focal point for the entire franchise. Dan Geraci, President and CEO of Phoenix Investments Partners, Ltd., likens them to "captains of sports teams in that they represent both the internal team and the management of the franchise itself. They have to do the right thing for both constituencies. Thus they are both a captain and a coach for the team." In other words, MVPs don't simply share the vision of the company; they mediate among different constituencies, ensuring that everyone furthers that vision. Gerry Lupacchino of Novations/J. Howard & Associates speaks of what can happen in the absence of the commitment typical of MVPs. "There are people that have worked with me in other organizations that consistently disparaged leadership. And the energy they spent positioning leadership in that way negatively impacted their productivity."

Through their tremendous faith in the company and their corresponding willingness to do what it's going to take to support leadership, MVPs exert a positive influence.

Tom Kochan of MIT sees MVPs encouraging everyone's commitment to company values and vision. Whether faculty or support staff, he says, MVPs are conscientious citizens and leaders. They inspire confidence in others; they know how to get things done; they ensure that major issues are resolved;

and, above all, "they have a deep commitment to the values of the place." Those values principally involve "helping people do their best work" by respecting "the fact that leadership comes at all levels of the organization and that leadership is not tied to some official position or high-level position of power in the organization is important to being an MVP." An MVP, in short, can recognize the commitment of subordinates and accept their contributions. That, too, is part of their investment in the company vision.

Not all MVPs express their commitment by being strong team players, however. Diane Hessan, President and CEO of Communispace, talks about one of her critical but sometimes challenging MVPs. "There are problems with what he does. He doesn't talk very much. He's a pain in the ass to work with. He's one of the original people in the company, but I am totally thrilled because he adds so much. On top of it all, he's so committed to the company that even with all his idiosyncrasies he produces great value. Some of it is talent, some of it is commitment. Some of it is just what I need in this culture. We're an entrepreneurial organization, so I need people to help me out by stepping forward and, on top of whatever else they do, just do it. These people are just going above and beyond and it's not because they are trying to suck up, but they just get it."

MVPs Enhance the Company's Reputation

MVPs bring in more business to the organization because of their reputation. We were told that clients, customers and people in similar and other industries will talk about these players and say how good they are. "Good" refers both to the results they achieve and to their stature and presence. People will say that these people are the best people to deal with; that they are fair, honest and open; and that they express and exemplify the values of the organization openly.

As Dan Geraci of Phoenix Investment Partners notes, "The prime indicator is the external and internal reactions to these people. Clients and people outside the business will talk about these players and will say how good they are, and want to do business with them. Internal people and colleagues also know they are very talented."

One executive also indicates that the reaction of customers is one of the key indicators of an MVP. "One of the first indicators for me in any business I've been involved with is the feedback I get from the customers, whether it's retail customers or institutional customers. It's unsolicited feedback you look for. It's not when you just walk up to someone and say, 'I know you work with Bill or Mary. What do think of them?' It's when they seek you out and they go out of their way through an email, handwritten note or a phone call with regard to how valuable this person is."

There are two value-added aspects to MVPs receiving external recognition. Some of the value that they produce is in the form of goodwill or public relations for the company. Because of their stature and public recognition they are able to bring further business to the organization. For instance, well-known and successful portfolio managers with financial services companies often bring in more assets because they are publicly recognized in terms of who they are and what they do. Their public stature will further enhance the reputation of the company, so there is a trickle-down effect for the rest of the organization.

MVPs Earn the Respect of Colleagues

A closely related characteristic of MVPs is that they earn the respect of colleagues. For colleagues they embody the best of the organization. Others see them as consistent, trustworthy and passionate people who give themselves over completely to projects they believe in, challenge the value of doubtful projects and always fulfill their promises.

One sign that someone is an MVP is the pleasure a co-worker feels when he or she is promoted. As Helen Sayles of Liberty Mutual points out, "the true test of a corporate MVP is if you were to put their name in the headlines of the company newsletter about a promotion or a significant accomplishment, there wouldn't be a whole lot of disagreement. Also it's what we call the newspaper test—if you get to read about their promotion in the national or local newspaper, would everyone go 'YES'? I think with MVPs people would say YES!"

The "good guys" aren't just people who perform well. MVPs are also recognized for their qualities as human beings. Gordon Bethune of Continental Airlines describes his trust in his top five people in the following way: "I could give them all my money and ask them to hold it for me. You don't have to worry about those people. But that's after years of working with somebody that you just respect and you trust. It's not just one thing, it's a million things." What's interesting in Bethune's comments is the way he characterizes his trust. He means, of course, that he trusts their professional performance, but expresses the strength of his feelings by emphasizing their personal integrity—he would trust them with his wallet!

How long does it take to earn trust and respect? Amanda Feve, a highly regarded Planner at J. Walter Thompson in New York City, provides a good example. We spoke with Amanda the day before she moved to the JWT London office. We asked her what she sees as the foundation of her career success, and her response was "I consider myself an absolute anomaly in terms of willingness to stick to one thing. And I think that may be a combination of humility and pragmatism; doing great work is definitely at the forefront of my mind. I think that from the time that I started here, I believed that if I was doing good work that it would ultimately be rewarded and recognized and that things would work out in the long run. I knew that there would be some sort of short-term sacrifices to be made. I've always been a very hard worker and I've always seen that work meet with results." We should tell you that Amanda has spent her entire professional career at JWT.

"The best" are dynamic and outgoing and when you see their work habits, you can trust them. They have integrity and they take the business seriously. Jim Miller of FiRE + iCE uses one word to describe an MVP's main personality characteristic: maturity. Keith Brown, FiRE + iCE's COO, agrees and adds that their opinions are respected because they have a good track record. They've earned that respect.

Checklist to Identify the Basic Traits of the MVP

Here is a checklist to help further determine who is an MVP in terms of the basic traits and qualities.

✓ MVPs are motivated to succeed and to achieve ever-improving results. They constantly need to raise the bar on their performance and always want to do better.

✓ They always want to succeed and never like to fail.

✓ MVPs are the people who always show moral courage and are not afraid to make the tough decisions.

✓ MVPs share and constantly demonstrate the vision and values of the organization.

✓ MVPs represent the company well both internally and externally and consequently are spoken of highly by people who deal with them. This, in turn, brings further goodwill to the organization.

✓ MVPs earn the respect of their colleagues and are known as people who demonstrate high integrity.

CHAPTER 4

卍

Managing the MVP

A few years ago, a subsidiary of an international company promoted its Chief Operating Officer to run the local operations because he was a very skillful businessman and was remarkably good at people management. At the time of his promotion to Chief Executive Officer, the company was still fairly small and was beginning to establish its reputation in the local market. Under the leadership of the new CEO, the company made rapid and positive gains. Within the space of two years, it was first in sales in the industry, won numerous awards for its products and customer service and was on the list of Best Companies to Work For. Its profitability was also the highest in relation to the other subsidiaries in the company.

In spite of all these achievements, the CEO never felt that he was valued by the parent company. He received the appropriate bonuses and stock options but never got feedback that what he was doing was valued or that he had a bright future with the international company.

Because he was viewed as an MVP in the local market, he received numerous calls from executive recruiters. His feelings of being undervalued grew to the point that he decided to apply for one of the opportunities that was presented to him and became CEO of another company in the industry.

When he left his former company, the successes that had been achieved over the last two years began to quickly evaporate. A person was brought in from the parent company to head up the subsidiary, but he did not understand the local culture or way of doing business. Within a few months, the company's sales had dropped dramatically, the company was downsized and morale was so bad that the company did not even apply to be on the Best Companies to Work For list for the next three years. All this happened because the CEO had not felt that he was valued!

Another case is that of Rick, who was hired as Production Manager of a manufacturing company from one of the market leaders in the industry. Rick quickly proved to be a valuable resource to the management team and improved production by 30 percent in the first year and by an additional 40 percent in both his second and third years. He was promoted to a senior production management job and was viewed by the Vice President of Manufacturing as an MVP with a bright future in the company.

The VP of Manufacturing was identified by the CEO as his successor, and he in turn confided in Rick that he wanted him to take over his position when he was promoted. About six months earlier than his scheduled retirement, the current CEO had a debilitating heart attack and was forced to retire. The VP of Manufacturing took over his position and was quickly swamped by the work. He soon appointed a COO—Frank—from outside, who had been recommended by one of the Board members. Frank was decisive but was not a good listener.

Frank made Rick feel like an order taker. When Rick put forward ideas for improvement, Frank rebuffed them. Also, Rick noticed that Frank began to cut him out of the decision-making loop and he felt that he was no longer valued or trusted. The CEO became aware that Rick was not happy and had a word with Frank about the situation. Frank's treatment of Rick did improve for a short while, until a major customer began to complain about service and support. Frank reverted back to his style of sharply worded orders and threats and began to blame Rick and all his peers for the situation.

Rick worked long and hard for the company and was rarely at home with his family. One day Frank questioned Rick's commitment to the company when Rick asked for an extended weekend to take his family for a short vacation, and this proved to be the "last straw" for Rick. He tendered his resignation and quickly became COO of a small manufacturing company. Many of his best employees left to join him at the new company. Once Rick left the former company, the production group began to fall apart. Frank was eventually fired and the CEO figured that the company had lost three years of growth and never recovered its momentum in the marketplace.

These stories illustrate that knowing how to manage MVPs is critical. If an organization is to achieve its mission and goals, it must keep its MVPs motivated. Failing to do so, as Dan Geraci, President and CEO of Phoenix Investment Partners, explains, carries demonstrable risks. "You don't want to become the training ground for someone else in your industry where your people rise to a certain level of competency and then say, 'Well, I'm done here, there is nothing more for me here, and I'll go across the street and be a hero.' Keeping them motivated, keeping them happy, keeping them stabilized becomes incredibly challenging." MVPs should be regarded as a precious resource that requires careful management.

How, then, should MVPs be managed? Some organizations assume that the best MVP management is no management. Simply leave them alone; as big boys and girls, MVPs can figure it out for themselves. Managers may believe that these top people are above requiring support or should be indulged. Some organizations believe that all people need to be treated the same, irrespective of whether they are MVPs or not. They may worry that affording MVPs special treatment risks inflating their egos. Some organizations may simply forget about the importance of managing people, whether MVPs or others. They are often too busy chasing business results to worry about the needs of personnel. Our interviews with companies that manage talent well show that MVPs need to be actively managed, but in a way different from the management of other people in the organization. They need to know that what they are doing has meaning, and that they are making a contribution. This is not just a job for them! They want to be part of a winning team and have a coach and leader that cares for them and is able to provide the resources and support they need. It must be noted that MVPs may be very talented and may be high performers, but to be truly successful they *do* need to know and learn the organization's basics, the technical aspects, etc. Leaving them completely to their own devices just because they're smart and motivated is not a good idea.

During the course of our interviews, six key themes emerged addressing the prerequisites for successfully managing the MVP. These are consistent with our experiences as both internal and external consultants to numerous organizations that have MVPs.

- develop an appropriate culture to allow the MVP to be productive and motivated. This includes making sure that the total compensation of the MVP is appropriate to the value they create
- adopt a management style that allows the MVP to produce and grow
- provide career development and feedback
- provide the MVP with challenge
- allow for flexibility
- encourage the MVP to stay

These themes do not operate in isolation—they are part of an integrated package. As Osbert Hood, formerly COO and now CEO of Pioneer Investments, tells us, "I like being in a great working environment, with very market-competitive compensation and receiving positive feedback from the company for what I do. I think it's a total package. It's like saying, which part of the total car can you take out and still have a functioning and reliable automobile? I think the environment, the relationship with the immediate supervisor and the compensation are all important in creating a balanced atmosphere."

Develop an Appropriate Culture to Allow the MVP to Be Productive and Motivated

MVPs cannot thrive in splendid isolation. Their happiness and productivity depend in large part on the surrounding culture, which in turn depends greatly on the leadership of the CEO. CEOs must create an environment in which MVPs feel that their job has meaning, that their contributions are recognized and that the organization treats them fairly. While nurturing such a culture is clearly important to encouraging the best efforts of all employees, it has special significance for promoting loyalty among MVPs. MVPs who feel alienated from an organization's culture and values will simply move on. There will always be another organization more sympathetic to their needs willing to take them in.

This section will cover:

- the role of the CEO in creating the culture
- the importance of providing a meaningful role
- the need for recognition, fairness and compensation appropriate to the value that the MVP creates

The Role of the CEO in Creating the Culture

CEOs are uniquely placed to create the conditions in which MVPs can thrive. They set the tone for the entire organization. As he describes in his book, *From Worst to First*, Gordon Bethune, Chairman and CEO of Continental Airlines, was able to turn the troubled company around in part because of his success in introducing a winning culture at Continental.[1] Bethune went to extraordinary lengths to create a culture where **every employee** feels that he or she is part of a winning team. One of his key principles is to make sure that when the team wins, everyone wins. He says, "If you are on the team, then you need to be a part of the team. This is the team we're going with. Screening out those that aren't and

---

[1] Gordon Bethune, *From Worst to First: Behind the Scenes of Continental's Remarkable Comeback* (John Wiley & Sons Inc., 1999).

won't be part of the team helps when you get infighting and turf war crap. I'm not going to tolerate that. You'll be gone just like the other 25 guys." As CEO, Bethune is in a position to set the firm's cultural agenda.

CEO Dan Geraci talks more directly about his culture-defining role. "My role becomes managing the managers, managing the environment, managing the motivation, setting the longer-term strategy. I think we should all manage in the fashion in which we like to be managed and all too often that's not the case." Of the cultures he has fostered in a number of organizations, he says, "I think a lot of what we've done around personal development issues, mission, vision, values, and the emphasis on charitable giving and community involvement says as much about what we stand for as anything else, and your talented people rise to the surface in an environment like that. If you don't put the right behavior and modeling in place at the top and cascade that down, you are never going to attract the right people, you are never going to retain them when you do have them, and you sure as hell aren't going to develop them. CEOs should define the firm." The CEO, in short, plays a critical role in creating the culture where the MVPs and their managers can succeed.

The Importance of Providing a Meaningful Role

We also heard from many MVPs on the importance of having a role they find genuinely meaningful. For MVPs, work must be more than the fulfillment of a narrowly defined set of tasks. It must be about more than themselves. They need to see that they are contributing to a larger enterprise, that their efforts are of benefit to all key stakeholders—in short, that their role has significance within a broader context. To help their MVPs thrive, then, organizations must promote a culture in which everyone, including the MVP, is made to feel the significance of his or her contribution to the greater good.

In some cases, creating that culture entails little more than fulfilling the organization's mandate. David Lissy, CEO of Bright Horizons Family Solutions, notes of his organization that "People who come to work for us from other places look around and think they have died and gone to heaven. They find a company that actually has a mission that they really live; people are passionate about working here. There's a real support network and we make decisions in careful, thoughtful ways, putting the children and families first. In all the things here, we walk the talk. We do it because I think it is important in every company to have a sense of culture, something that makes you feel good working here." Bright Horizons Family Solutions strives to improve the lives of children and families. As long as the company fulfills its mission, MVPs are bound to appreciate the significance of their role. Ann Pickens, Vice President, Strategic Planning at Bright Horizons, tells us that the most important aspect of work for her is that she really loves what she is doing. "I chose this field and this company deliberately [early childhood education and corporate child care]. I feel respected by the people I work with, customers and co-workers, and I respect them."

In other cases, however, the MVPs need to be reminded of that significance more actively. John Humphrey, once Chairman of Forum and now Chairman of a volunteer non-profit arts organization, comments on precisely this imperative. "You continuously frame the issue in the sense that they are doing work that has meaning for them and meaning for other people and for the world in general." During his tenure as Chairman at Forum, the company had a reputation among its employees as being the "Best Place I Know to Learn and Grow." Humphrey attributes the spread of that reputation to the contract that he had with staff acknowledging the importance of their work and their personal growth.

Of course, in creating an MVP-friendly culture, more than simple acknowledgement is required. The MVP's role must be genuinely significant. Again, in some instances, the nature of the business itself conveys that significance. John Hatsopoulos, who used to head up Thermo Electron, tells us of the effect that the company's artificial heart project had on employees. "This did so much for the morale of the employees because they were proud. The revenues of Thermo Electron in 1998, which was the last year I was President, were US$4.5 billion. The revenues from the artificial heart were just coming in and they were US$15 million to US$20 million. If you asked any of the employees what the company manufactured, they would say the artificial heart. And these were people working in divisions related to making products and services for the environment, cleaning up water, building power plants and the rest. But the production of the artificial heart was their pride and joy."

In the absence of such a self-evidently important rallying point, leadership must be proactive. Mark Howes, Vice President, Mechanical Systems and Accessories at Honeywell, talks about creating a compelling purpose for what his organization is trying to accomplish and making it an attractive place for MVPs. He notes that MVPs "are going to move and be in high demand, and they're going to grow, and they're going to be called upon to take on other roles. I try to make their work in the division interesting and compelling so that people will feel that this is important to our business. I need to make sure that this is a good place to be, and that it is an attractive place for other high-potential folks. I want to ensure that high-potential folks know about how things are being done here and would like to be a part of it, so that we can keep more of those kinds of people coming into the business."

The Need for Recognition and Compensation Appropriate to the Value the MVP Creates

Providing MVPs with due recognition and fair treatment are also key elements in the creation of a helpful culture. MVPs need to feel that their contributions are worth the effort and that they will get some form of recognition. Dan Geraci says, "You have to create an environment that encourages MVPs to shine, to step up. If people don't believe that there is any reward, that there is any point in going the extra step, in going beyond, they won't because no one likes to sit there and know that they are doing twice as much as the person next to them and getting no recognition for it."

Recognition can come in different forms. Often it's a matter of providing compensation that differentiates the high-performing individuals from other employees. Recognition can come in different forms. According to Mark Snyder, Global Head of Foreign Exchange and Money Markets for State Street Global Markets, "Some companies have a compensation philosophy that is unintentionally generic and does not sufficiently reward high-performance professionals relative to their counterparts at their competitors. A thoughtful, market-based compensation structure is a key part of delivering consistently high client service and generating shareholder value. Losing MVPs and other talented individuals due to compensation constraints will certainly limit the long-term growth prospects of a high-margin sell-side trading and sales franchise. Compensation policies for bonuses and stock incentives must therefore be dispassionate and carefully constructed in order to consistently achieve high goals."

But compensation isn't always solely the issue. As Tim Manning, Senior Vice President of HR at NSTAR says, "Oftentimes, recognition comes in multiple forms, not only in the form of money, but in the form of incentive compensation, rewards or even just separate conversations about recognizing personal achievement. I personally subscribe to Maslow's theory on those things: if you take care of safety and security needs and those kinds of issues, people truly are focused and their attention is on making a difference, and they aren't really worried about losing what they have or are even concerned about it; they're just focused on an outcome. If that is threatened in any way, shape or form in terms of rewards systems, then people will have a tendency to regress." Robin Burns, President and CEO of Intimate Beauty Corporation, also comments on multiple forms of recognition. "I am very high on recognizing people for any contribution or work that they do. I think that that is a big part of retention and it can be by simple things. It can be a hand-written note. It can be publicly acknowledging them. It can be financially rewarding them. It could be a myriad of things. But I think consistency of that recognition is something that really makes people feel appreciated and valued."

Recognition, it should be noted, doesn't necessarily mean making stars out of MVPs. Liberty Mutual pays MVPs well, but according to Helen Sayles won't "put a gold star on their forehead. We are not an elitist organization; we are a very practical organization displaying common sense. So, we don't want a star mentality. The MVPs will be stars because they are very good at what they do and because other people will recognize that they are, but we don't need to anoint them." Bright Horizons Family Solutions also will not tolerate a star mentality. According to Executive Chairman Roger Brown, Bright Horizons has "tried to create a culture that isn't star oriented and not a culture of bribes. In some organizations I've seen use of massive compensation to overcome everything else. I think that is negative, and requires you to pay twice—once with the paycheck and again with the fallout of entitlement and resentment. If you pay too much to some people, you make others disgruntled. Eventually these people who want more money will get a better offer and they will leave. If someone is in it purely for the money, they can be bought. I believe that when people are contributing, they know it and they feel good about it. When they know what they have done is good for a center, a child or the organization, that makes them feel good. I think, secondly, when you recognize their contribution directly, that feels great. You can recognize it with a bonus, or kind words or some kind of acknowledgement. Again, if you know the person, you'll know what they might respond to. I've always believed in recognizing people publicly, not only because it makes them feel good but because it gives everyone else a sense of what the company likes and rewards."

Checklist on How to Create an Appropriate Culture

It sounds obvious, but it is the senior leader who needs to create the culture that encourages the MVP to be productive and stay. What do they have to do?

✓ Constantly solicit MVPs' ideas for improvement, and where appropriate implement them. Don't feel you have to know everything and make all the decisions, even though you have talented people working for you.

✓ Don't feel threatened by MVPs. They are true team players and will make you look good as long as you value their contribution.

✓ Give meaning to their work and role, whether it be in terms of the importance of the products and services they are providing to the market, or that they are developing other people around them. Explain to them how they fit in to providing products and services and give them feedback on the results that the company is achieving in the industry and the community.

✓ Make sure that MVPs achieve appropriate recognition for the value they are bringing to the company. Ensure that they receive higher bonuses and stock options than people who are providing less value. This does not always happen since some managers are afraid to differentiate compensation awards on the basis of performance, for fear of upsetting people.

✓ Ensure that MVPs receive recognition in forms other than compensation. Give them frequent feedback that they are valued; make sure that they are thanked when they produce extraordinary results, whether privately or in public. Don't assume that they automatically know that they are doing a good job. MVPs are human too!

Adopt a Management Style That Allows the MVP to Produce and Grow

Our interviews reveal that both MVPs and their managers think that three things are important to the management of the MVP:

- providing the MVP with clear direction on strategy and the results required
- delegating authority to the MVP
- developing a relationship with the MVP

While these elements are important to most employees, they have added significance for MVPs. The managers of MVPs have to assume that MVPs are competent and talented and do not need to be micromanaged. Micromanagement is likely to turn them off and cause them to look for positions elsewhere, or to become troublesome. This does not mean, however, that they should be left completely to their own devices, since they need to be given a clear path to follow.

Providing the MVP with Clear Direction on Strategy and the Results Required

The role of the manager is to ensure that MVP goals are clearly defined. MVPs must be able to see that the required results will genuinely help the organization. Because MVPs like autonomy and can sometimes see things differently from their colleagues, it is important that the manager and the MVP do the goal setting in a collaborative manner. MVPs need to have their opinions and thoughts on direction valued and taken into consideration. Once goals have been set, the manager has the delicate task of giving the MVP autonomy to achieve these goals, while ensuring that the MVP is kept focused and on track. This delicacy is best handled by discussing expectations directly with the MVP before a manager's oversight is required.

Ned Riley, Chief Investment Strategist at SSgA, talks clearly about autonomy and his role in managing the MVPs. "I like the MVPs to come up with the ideas for success. It's not me sitting there in an isolated ivory tower saying this is the way it should be done. In this way you basically get buy-in for the strategic direction, and the majority of the time it will be consistent with your own if it's a pretty good program. So there is less of them dictating to me; it is more of them deciding that these are the areas we should focus on. I like to provide wisdom when they think it's necessary, to provide some experiences when I think they are needed, but not interfere so much that it totally disrupts strategic direction. There are situations that I can fall back on so that I can share my experience with them and I can share the apparent solutions at that time. It doesn't mean it will always be the same, but I really believe that a good group works on its own issues, on its own problems."

A CEO who manages numerous MVPs uses the analogy of managing an eager and spirited racehorse. "The most important thing for me to do in managing talented people is really to keep them going and to give them a path. The analogy that I use is that of a racehorse because I have worked with very spirited and eager racehorses. My role, I find, as a leader of these MVPs is to make sure that I don't interrupt the oval or the track, but it's basically when they start to jump over the fence to get off the track…that's when I do something about it. It's not to slow them down, but it's to keep them on target and I try to do that very consciously. I find that that's the most efficient way of getting the most out of those people and at the same time, keeping them focused on what they are supposed to do, which is a master plan that involves a lot of these MVPs and others. So, it's more encouragement than steering business on my part, because if I hire correctly then I'm hiring people who eventually and hopefully quickly get what we are trying to do."

Delegating Authority to the MVP

MVPs must be given direction but MVPs also typically want independence. According to Gordon Bethune, they "want the autonomy to do the job." Speaking of his own experience, Ned Riley of SSgA explains, "I actually value the freedom, the independence, the notion that there's more than one way to solve a problem. Nobody has a monopoly on the ideas." The challenge for managers is to grant their MVPs autonomy while still providing oversight and support.

The dangers of micromanaging MVPs are real. Stan Shelton of State Street is very clear on not managing talent too tightly. "Valuable people are valuable because they do their role without any real need for oversight. I think as managers we just coordinate. It's really coordinating across the enterprise with respect to talent and this is a large part of my role. I delegate goals as part of my role. The open environment allows them to do what they do so well, and to tie the components back into the bigger strategy and objectives that we're seeking to achieve. You certainly don't try to know everything that's going on. Otherwise, you're not doing your job very well."

Amanda Feve, who works at J. Walter Thompson as a Brand Planner, notes, "The best way to manage me is to trust that I'm going to do what I have to do. I find that the best way for me is let me get my work done and when it's done just sit down and talk about it. I don't appreciate micromanagerial tendencies."

"I think one of the reasons why I'm still here is they let me run with the ball and do great work," is the thought of Ed Evangelista, an Executive Creative Director of JWT in New York, on how he works best with his managers. "I think that's important also for the kinds of people that you hire and for the kinds of people who want to be MVPs. I think you have to be able to be handed the ball and be able to run with it and not be afraid. You either sink or swim, based on your actions. That's the secret."

MVPs need to be supported rather than controlled. The experiences of Mark Howes of Honeywell illustrate this point precisely. "I find a number of folks who are willing to go out and make things happen. They need to talk about it. They need somebody to exchange with. And they need someplace to just express their views and their concerns, maybe even express some insecurity, in a safe environment. And they don't necessarily need to be told how to do things. They just need to know that there's support and there's acknowledgement and there's somebody that's with them and is there to help." Kevin Wassong of J. Walter Thompson concurs. "I like to be given a very clear-cut goal and then a time frame to get there. I've been given the freedom to fly here and that's what's been exciting about it. I think what keeps people really motivated is when you give them a task and give them a time frame and know that they are fully capable of it and help redirect them at times. Essentially, that's the yardstick for success."

Developing a Relationship with the MVP

Managers must get to know their MVPs and pay attention to their needs. The responsibilities placed on managers are often so heavy and various that they may feel they have little time for mere get-to-know-you sessions, yet such sessions are invaluable to the proper management of MVPs. As one interviewee notes, "You have to be extra attentive to MVPs and meet some or all of their demands in order to be assured, or have a reasonable likelihood, of keeping them. You need to know what is important to the individual. Because a person could be lured away by the promise of a parking spot, somebody else could be lured away by the promise of a corner office, somebody else could be lured away by dollars and cents, somebody else could be lured away by international travel, somebody else could be lured away by the fact that they see it as a trajectory to the CEO's office. You need to know what's going to make the difference with that person."

One great advantage of making the effort to meet with MVPs is that MVPs themselves can provide insight on how best to manage them. Mike Hyter, CEO of Novations/J. Howard & Associates, notes that "Each one of us, as individuals, has interests and things that mobilize or stimulate us that are different from what might mobilize or stimulate someone else." According to John Marrs, Senior Vice President of Human Resources for State Street Bank, MVPs are likely to reveal their particular motivations and needs on their own. Management must only listen. Marrs advises, "Make sure you pay attention to them. They'll tell you what to do for them, because they are MVPs. They've thought about it and they know."

Many of the executives that we spoke to recommended having a regularly scheduled meeting with individual MVPs to find out how things are going, what is on their mind and how they can be supported. Diane Hessan, CEO of Communispace, advises managers to "schedule a time to meet with the MVP to talk about the future. The goal is to let him or her know you've decided that he or she has enormous potential in the organization and you would like to formally begin a process to make sure that he or she is getting the development that is needed to be able to move up in the organization. That can take a number of forms: meeting with your MVPs more often, spending time listening to what your MVPs believe needs to happen in the department, the division, the company. These people also crave feedback—both positive and negative—and so we work to be very specific in this area." Meetings might take the form of breakfast, lunch or dinner meetings over the course of a few months. Barbara Piehler, Senior Vice President and Chief Information Officer for Northwestern Mutual, ensures that she meets her MVPs and all her managers regularly in an informal setting during the course of a year. For others, it can be an unscheduled meeting when the person needs to talk. Whatever the method, the need to meet regularly is a prerequisite to getting to know the MVP well.

Knowing an MVP well is very important as a means of retaining the individual in the organization. Managers must be clear on such things as:

- what people are looking for in their job
- where they are looking to go in terms of future opportunities
- what they are looking for in career development
- how as a manager you can help them get there

Failing to strive for clarity on such issues risks losing your MVPs.

Career Development and Feedback

Managers need to develop their MVPs if MVPs are to take on greater organizational responsibility and if organizations are to benefit from MVP talent in full. This section will cover:

- the role of the manager in the development process
- moving MVPs at an appropriate pace
- providing feedback

The Role of the Manager in the Development Process

One of the key roles of any leader is to ensure that a talent pool exists to fulfill the succession needs of the organization. This will prevent the dependence of the organization on the leader and a few MVPs whose departure would be disastrous for future success of the business. The manager, therefore, needs to coach the current MVPs on how to ensure their own success, and also on how to develop and strengthen other potential MVPs in order to ensure that there is a vibrant talent pool.

Those who believed strongly in the developmental process said that the role of the CEO and manager is to work with MVPs. As Helen Sayles of Liberty Mutual comments, "This involves encouraging them, making them feel good about what they are doing, and being very constructive in criticizing them when criticism is the only way." Another CEO tells us, "What I have to do is to keep them [MVPs] motivated positively in terms of feeling that they can achieve outstanding results. I need to give them all the tools and resources and positive feedback that I can. I also need to open the door for them to get to where we decide that they should be going. If they don't get to where they should be, I then spend some time with them and focus on changing direction for them, or coaching them on the area where they need development." Those managers that believe in the development of their MVPs act as teachers to the people that work for them and are different from the managers who basically pay people to perform a duty for them.

One of the key roles of the manager in developing MVPs is to look for growth and development opportunities for them. This means putting their name forward for company-wide projects and assignments, or mentioning their names as potential candidates for other opportunities in the organization. This is counterintuitive to numerous managers who may refuse to identify their MVPs because they do not want people who bring value to their section to leave and go to another part of the organization. They even give them lower performance ratings so that other managers will not pick them off!

But Simon Wilson-Taylor, Managing Director and Senior Vice President of Global Link at State Street, talks about developing his best people by finding opportunities for them outside of his business area. We asked Simon if he might hesitate in doing this to protect his area's productivity. He responds that "That would be a very short-term view. And in fact, I think it's even wrong in the short term, because by giving one individual the opportunity to do something different you are showing others that anything is possible. And that inspires everybody else to achieve more and greater things."

When managers are serious about developing an MVP, they may risk placing that person in a position that stretches him or her. Mike Hyter of Novations/J. Howard & Associates recalls being placed in such a position at his former company, a large retail organization. Even though his background was strictly in HR, he was asked to move over to store management by his mentor, the company CEO. "The CEO said to me, 'Have you thought about running a business?' I never thought it would be possible, because I'm an HR person by training and by experience. I'd never trained to be a [retail] store manager. He said, 'We have a store manager opening, it's in Lansing, Michigan, and it would mean having to move back to Michigan.' I was living in Minneapolis at the time. He said, 'It's a US$23 million business with only 200 employees. It would be a wonderful opportunity if you were interested because it would just give you another dimension of our business.'" The CEO made one invaluable promise to him when he put him in an area out of his immediate area of competency.

He said, "And I won't let you fail." This was especially important to Mike since he is a professional of color. The CEO never had to do anything to keep him from failing, but this statement alone provided Mike with confidence.

Are You Overlooking an Important Source of Potential MVPs?

By Mike Hyter, President and CEO of Novations/
J. Howard & Associates

In my consulting work with large corporations all across the country, I often hear aspiring, hard-working women and professionals of color say that they have to work harder to be recognized, that they too often get excluded from informal networks where one learns the inner workings of an organization, and that even when their contributions are significant they are less likely to be tapped for positions of leadership.

I wish I could say their perceptions were always unfounded but, unfortunately, my experience is that women and professionals of color too often get tapped for challenging opportunities only *after* they've proven themselves time and time again. In contrast, their equally hard-working and ambitious white male counterparts are more likely to be given opportunities based on their *potential* ("He hasn't done anything like this before, but I know he'll come through for us."). Since in my opinion, it's this succession of "at bats" and the confidence about one's talents displayed by people in power that accelerate the development of MVPs, motivated women and people of color often *do* have to work harder just to be given a chance to play the game.

I'm not saying that this is a *deliberate* strategy on the part of senior leaders. Rather, I think most managers today are eager to accelerate the development of a broad range of talented individuals. It is, therefore, an unconscious outcome of the human tendency to be more comfortable and trusting of people who are similar to ourselves.

My advice to those charged with building the bench strength of your organizations: Examine your own filters. Do all of the folks who "rise to the top" resemble you in race, gender and background? If the answer is yes, don't assume that this homogeneity is merely a reflection of the best talent that could be found. *Challenge yourself to consider what talent is being missed.* Look a little more closely at those hardworking individuals who might lie outside your radar screen. Is there some motivated man or woman who just needs the same key assignments, informal coaching and straight feedback you're giving others in the organization with whom you're more comfortable?

I also have some advice for the young woman or professional of color. Don't let up on your efforts—or let first-pass rejections kill your spirit. Be dogged in pursuing opportunities to positively impact the business. Be willing to take the risks involved in key assignments; accept the challenge of the thorny problems the business most needs solved.

Understand that such risk-taking brings the certainty of occasional failure. Develop the resilience to view those setbacks as nothing more than information about how to be more successful the next time around. Reach out and make the interpersonal connections that give you access to the "inside information." Let people get to know *you* and how you think. Show that you are "relationship worthy." Build trust that you can be depended on to further your manager's interests and the interests of the business in critical situations.

In my opinion, every MVP is a product of preparation, coaching and opportunities to play in the "big game." Players of all backgrounds have the responsibility to put in the strategic, focused effort to learn how to contribute at the highest levels. Managers have the responsibility to work through their discomfort with differences, provide challenging assignments to a broader pool of individuals, and give honest, supportive coaching. The payoff is a team that truly uses the full range of talent available.

Unfortunately, a number of managers may not want to develop their MVPs because they feel intimidated by them. Because of their own insecurity, these managers are unwilling to allow people to rise to their level or above. Sometimes these managers want personal recognition for the achievement of results and are not willing to share that recognition with any of their staff and particularly their MVPs. Such managers must realize that they will be recognized for helping to develop and cultivating MVPs. They will be recognized for helping them achieve what is right for the organization.

Mentoring the MVP

Mentoring the MVP is an important way to successfully manage, retain and develop MVPs; often better than more traditional management techniques. John Humphrey remembers learning this lesson from Bob Timmins, the coach of Jim Ryan, who broke the high school mile record. Jim Ryan was in 9th grade and went to try out as a track sprinter and was cut and never ran in a race. In 10th grade he became a quarter miler. In the junior year he moved up to the mile and won the state, and in his senior year he broke the high school record. He then went on to be one of the great milers this country had ever seen. As Humphrey says, "Timmins had this theory about developing talent. I thought it was about finding your event. I use this theory, and in finding the event for your talented folks you've got to watch a lot of people, you've got to try a lot of things. I would tell talented people to spend a lot of time looking at people, and trying things out, and testing things out, and I would encourage them to put themselves in positions where they will be tested. Also I would tell them to create obligations for themselves that will drag them into performing situations, and then seek feedback. The next thing I would say is find a mentor. Choose that mentor carefully. You've got to find a mentor who is in that event. If you have the right event and you have someone interested in you, it's mostly a matter of chemistry."

Mentors: Who Are They and What Do They Do for MVPs?

Mentors are respected people in an organization who are valued for their experience, success and wisdom, and work with MVPs on a formal basis to help them learn how to be even more successful in the organization. They usually work in the company or are people with relevant experience who are hired by the company to be mentors. The managers of MVPs can suggest the names of people in the organization who are available for mentoring or MVPs can find their own resources by talking to people in the Human Resources department.

The specific roles that mentors play are to:

- help MVPs grow and develop by learning specific leadership and business skills
- help them navigate their way through the company culture and politics and gain credibility
- act as a coach and counselor
- be a sounding board for new ideas
- create opportunities for MVPs to use new skills

Mentors are most effective if they come from another part of the organization or from outside and have no direct responsibility for the management of the MVP. It is helpful if the organization has a stable of people that can be used as mentors, because it is important that the MVP and mentor fit well together and can form a strong learning partnership. The key factor is that there has to be good chemistry and fit between the MVP and the mentor in order for the MVP to learn and grow.

Often a mentor is appointed to work with the MVP for a period of 12 months. Usually, mentoring meetings take place for an hour-and-a-half on a monthly basis. Often there are informal meetings in between when the MVP needs some specific advice from his or her mentor and sometimes this relationship carries on for many years on an informal basis. The mentor needs to find out as much as possible about the MVP before he or she begins the mentoring sessions. This relates to both company and personal issues and can cover such areas as:

- structure and roles of the MVP's organization and the key players in it
- the MVP's successes, failures and likely areas for development
- required results and goals to be achieved
- personal background and management preferences
- values that are important to the MVP

Once the mentoring sessions begin, the MVP and the mentor need to be clear about what they expect from each other and the results they hope to achieve, and define ways to determine if the mentoring process is producing the required results. The MVP also has to commit to follow the suggestions and ideas that the mentor puts forward and that they jointly agree on.

Some of the specific areas that the MVP and mentor are likely to want to cover and produce actions plans for are:

- how to create appropriate strategic and business plans and make sure that the required results are achieved
- the makeup of the company organization and politics and how to build credibility
- the work ethics of the organization
- how to manage or improve interpersonal and management skills
- the decision-making process and how to be successful at making and implementing decisions
- how to manage the financial aspects of the role

- how to keep up to date with industry news and trends
- how to improve presentation skills—written and oral
- how to successfully negotiate in the company

Make sure that the MVP and the mentor regularly assess the usefulness of the mentoring relationship to ensure that both parties feel that it is producing the required results. Such an assessment is particularly useful at the end of the formal process that has been agreed to. This will help the mentor to learn how to further enhance his or her future mentoring relationships.

It must be noted that in turn, MVPs can also be a resource to mentor other people in the organization. True MVPs are respected in the organization and are willing to develop others. The value that MVPs bring to the organization will be greatly enhanced if they are given some time to mentor others and to teach and coach them how to bring value to the organization. They can pass on many of the skills that they have learned as they have grown and become MVPs.

Moving MVPs at an Appropriate Pace

Managers need to be assured that their MVPs move at an appropriate pace. MVPs on the fast track may ultimately derail if they haven't first learned enough about the basic business, experienced being held accountable for results, or faced the challenge of performing a large job that stretches their capabilities.

Dan Geraci of Phoenix Investment Partners notes, "Once you give talented people recognition, they become aware of the fact that they are talented and there is this constant tug of war between developing them and moving them along and recognizing them fast enough." During our consulting assignments, we have seen many people who, having failed to gain sufficient experience in their previous roles, moved too fast into new opportunities. In such cases, the consequences for both the individual and the organization are almost always negative.

If these consequences are to be avoided, both MVPs and their managers must show patience. "It's the overconfidence," says Geraci, "that has to be kept in check. Where there is a lack of a formal program or track, people will tend to accelerate themselves far too quickly. And people around them will accelerate them too quickly. So, the biggest challenge is keeping them focused and motivated in the role they are in and helping them to develop that patience and necessary calm that allows them to become deeper in a particular role or responsibility rather than this shallower hit-and-run style of career-pathing. They have to be kept in a position long enough to experience failure and success and to learn something from it, not simply to get results. The higher up you move someone, the less on-the-job training you want them to have to go through in that position. The expectation is that they can have an immediate impact and if they aren't prepared, you are setting them up to fail. It's a corporate responsibility."

Providing Feedback

Managers must give MVPs honest feedback, both positive and negative, if they are to grow and develop. "Be honest about their development needs," advises Lou de Ocejo, Executive Vice President of Human Resources and Organizational Performance at State Street, "because they have them just like everyone else. Nobody is perfect. Sit them down and ask them what's on their mind. Be honest with them. Tell them you are getting the wrong vibes: are they not happy, are they uncomfortable, are they being approached? There is no better substitute than asking, and people will usually tell you the truth, by the way. If they don't tell you the truth, then you've also learned something new—that maybe they're not an MVP." Helen Sayles of Liberty Mutual uses the sports analogy with regard to providing feedback to MVPs. "The best coaches are the first ones, when someone is not doing what they have the potential for, to be right in their face and be very explicit. They are also the biggest supporters when things are going well. You can't help people improve if you don't point out where they could improve."

It is important to give feedback to talented people early in their careers, particularly if they are beginning to demonstrate behavior that may cause them to fail. Failure would be a great loss to the company! Jerry Bliley, the Vice Chairman of Spencer Stuart Canada, talks about people who early in their careers believe that brilliance is everything. They may be good at personally producing results, but do not have good relations with others and think that they have no peers in terms of intellect or achievements. "I think you just have to be brutally honest," says Bliley, "when managing potential MVPs. Some people that have got a long way in their career are still behaving in a way that will ultimately cause them to fail because somebody wasn't brutally honest with them. Usually this is around their relationship and people management skills. You can't redeem them all, but some people could be redeemed if their leaders said, 'I know you think you are smart as hell but if you can't get this done with people, you're never going to go anywhere.' They have to know how to get things done with people. I think that's the message that you need to give people when they are young. When they are 45, forget it."

Sharing honest feedback at any point in an MVP's career seems to be particularly difficult for many managers. They may not see it as part of their job, they may fear upsetting the individual or they may have legal concerns. Not giving MVPs open and honest feedback, however, is doing them a disservice. Unaware of their shortcomings, MVPs may carry on making mistakes that can ultimately cause derailment.

How Do You Give Honest Feedback?

✓ Collect specific examples of where the MVP needs to improve or do things differently. What is he or she doing or not doing? What are the indicators and measures that things need to be done differently?

✓ If necessary, collect information from other peers to verify your observations and examples and to get a better assessment.

✓ Set up a meeting time with the MVP to go over the feedback. Make sure the meeting is conducted in a businesslike and positive manner.

✓ Provide the MVP with honest feedback and ways to improve or do things differently so that he or she knows what suggestions you have for improvements and how these suggestions can be turned into action. Make sure you outline what improvements you would like, together with the required measures. Remember that MVPs are always looking to improve and like to measure their progress.

✓ Continue to meet with the MVP to assess progress and to coach him or her to success.

Provide the MVP with Challenge

Virtually every one of the people we spoke to in our numerous interviews noted that managers needed to provide challenge for the MVP. MVPs must be placed in challenging jobs and environments if they are to benefit not only themselves but the organization. This section will cover:

• providing the opportunities for challenge
• benefits to the organization

Providing the Opportunities for Challenge

Without challenge, MVPs get bored and sometimes even become troublesome. They need to be solving large problems or issues to remain motivated. Helen Sayles of Liberty Mutual notes, "MVPs want to be given the impossible and they will find a way to do it. They want to be constantly tested, and they want the opportunity to take something and make it their own, and again there's that notion of redefining the

role. They want to take the role and make it something different. They feel like they can really make a difference. For true
MVPs, it's not a grind. They love it and they have fun doing
it." Tim Manning of NSTAR makes a similar point. "You really
need to put them in jobs where they have opportunities to
make an impact because these high-potential folks are driven
towards a result and a result that adds value. If these folks are
engaged in something that really, in the overall scheme of
things, doesn't have a big impact, it's not going to be all that
interesting to them." Barbara Piehler of Northwestern Mutual
speaks from her perspective as an acknowledged MVP. "I like
the big challenges. Once I fix the big challenges—or I fix the
people problems and get the right people in the right jobs to
get things done—that's when I leave it behind and move on
to another challenge." This is consistent with what we heard
from many other MVPs. Once the challenge is fixed, give
them another large challenge or they get bored.

Benefits to the Organization

Providing challenge to the MVP is not only for the benefit of
the individual. It can also provide great results for the organization, so that it becomes a win-win situation for both the
individual and the organization. Ned Riley, an MVP at SSgA,
talks about the benefits to the organization of providing challenge to the MVPs and others. "I think the intellectual
stimulation and the search for the novel, the new, the exciting is very powerful. State Street is a very research-oriented
organization and it's research in a non-traditional way. It has
a whole group of individuals who are purely dedicated to the
development of different and unique ways of investing
money. And when it does develop a product, it's extremely
successful in selling it because of the results and the proven
track record of the particular product it is producing."

Challenging MVPs may mean putting them in a job beyond
their skills, so that they must ascend a steep learning curve.
This can pay great dividends to the company. John Marrs, also
at SSgA, shares the story of a person who needed a challenge

and ended up creating a potentially high-revenue-generating business. "There is a guy here who is very capable and I knew he was chomping at the bit to do something different. So, we put him in a job where he was totally out of what was the norm for him. No one even thought of his name for this job...but I knew from conversations with him that he was not feeling challenged anymore. So I recommended that we move him over into this different role. Once there, he came up with the idea of how to turn this business into something different than it was before. He looked at it from a much broader perspective. It was kind of an adjunct to a business before and now my prediction is that in the next year-and-a-half that will be a full-fledged revenue-generating business. All that from putting an MVP in that role."

Allow for Flexibility

We noted earlier that it was essential for the manager to spend time with his or her MVPs and to get to know them well. Part of knowing them well is being aware of their personal circumstances and the impact these circumstances can have on their work and motivation. In some cases it may be necessary to provide some creativity and flexibility in their work schedules to prevent them leaving the organization.

For example, long-time workers in danger of burning out may need to be given a sabbatical. John Humphrey tells us about a general manager who quit a not-for-profit organization after 12 years of hectic and complicated growth. Humphrey felt that this very talented person would have stayed with the organization if he had been given time to refresh himself.

Virginia Murray, Vice President and Managing Director of A.T. Kearney Executive Search in Toronto, tells a similar story of a person she tried to recruit away from a consulting firm. "He wasn't a senior, senior person but clearly an MVP of his team. He was going to leave the firm because of the large amount of travel he did. I had a great job for him and we gave him the offer. However, his current firm gave him a six-month sabbatical, and all the rest of us could say was, 'Good for you, isn't that great.' The consulting firm finally heard what his issue was. If they had offered him money it wouldn't have mattered. They said, 'Take six months and stay at home with your family. We'll create a job for you that doesn't require you to travel so much.' He is still with the organization."

Granting sabbaticals can sometimes involve benefits to the company beyond revitalizing an MVP. Sandy West, Executive Vice President of HR at Limited Brands, recounts the story of a very senior person in a multi-billion dollar organization who was given time off to pursue his educational dreams. "We had a gentleman who is leaving a significant function. He really wanted to have an opportunity to try for a role like Chairman and he also really wanted to get his Ph.D. We ensured hiring some terrific talent to allow him to be in a position to pursue his dream of getting a Ph.D. He is pursuing his educational dream, which, I think, will also help him be even more prepared should the opportunity be there for him to be in a COO/Vice Chair kind of role. He is one of several people in terms of critical talent at a CEO/President-type level in the total organization."

Being flexible doesn't have to be as dramatic as providing a sabbatical or an extended period of leave. It may be a case of providing the MVP with a flexible schedule. Mike Hyter of Novations/J. Howard & Associates describes how one of his VPs works a shorter week and yet still accomplishes amazing results for the company. "I can give you an example of one of my direct reports. She has a brilliant mind, is an excellent writer, is a very creative problem solver, and has a very strong relationship acumen. She's also a mother of two young children, is happily married and is very active in her faith. For the last two or three years she has taken two days off a week to take care of her kids. I named her Vice President of Operations and I've added Strategy recently. But I didn't expect her schedule to change because outcome is all I'm interested in. She is more productive on her work schedule than most people who work every day. But it's unorthodox in terms of our schedule. She and I might have one-on-one status sessions between 10:00 and 11:30 at night. We do have a lot of conversations on our cell phones. She is motivated by intellectual pursuit and making contributions to the success of the organization. Plus, she's also grateful that her family obligations are as important to me as they are to her."

Encourage the MVP to Stay

Many managers worry about what would happen to their business if their MVPs left. Reasons MVPs might want to leave include feeling blocked or undervalued or never being not told that they are valuable to the organization. It is better to ensure that MVPs do not want to leave in the first place. But once they raise the issue, it is important to find out why they are leaving and see if this can be prevented. Sandy West of Limited Brands talks about the great lengths the organization will go to try and keep an MVP. "If someone valuable says they are leaving, we would have a very open conversation, up to and including having Les—the Chairman—talk to people. We have a real belief that people join organizations and they leave people. We spend a lot of time trying to understand why they are leaving and why they see the other opportunity as better for them. A gentleman here was recruited away by an organization here in town. And part of the intrigue for him was they were telling him he would have a broader role. When we found out about this, we told him we wanted him to complete the interviews but that we were going to work on a way of providing him a broader role over the next six months. We were sure that as he went through the interview process he would actually become less interested in the job, and that is exactly what happened. In the meantime, we put together a plan to get his responsibilities broadened. It's going to occur in phases, and a phase of that has already happened. We also obviously took a look at his compensation, typical for probably most companies."

J. Walter Thompson is a leader in the advertising industry and is known to develop great talent. The agency works hard to identify and keep its best people in this very competitive business. Samantha Digennaro, Senior Partner and Director of Communications, recalls "being poached" by another agency. They had made her a very attractive offer. How did she decide to stay or to go? "I had a great heart-to-heart with Bob Jeffrey [the then President of North America], who also suggested that I talk to Megwin [Finegan, a Senior Partner]. What transpired in those conversations are two of the factors that ultimately led me to stay at JWT." Samantha knew and was guided toward the best, as in honest and trustworthy, resources within her company to seek out and discuss the pros and the cons of the offer. Knowing who to talk with when an attractive offer comes in is a critical tool that managers can give to an MVP before the need arises.

Building on many of the points we included earlier in the chapter, we have created a checklist of actions that may help managers dissuade an MVP from leaving. These actions can be effective even after an MVP begins receiving outside offers. It is preferable, however, to take these actions *before* the MVP receives such offers. To use this approach, the manager and the MVP must already have a relationship built on integrity and respect that will foster trust. Also, the MVP must be earning a market-competitive compensation package. If the compensation is not competitive, the manager's best option might be to throw money at the MVP and possibly beg them to stay! If both criteria are met, then the following approach will do much to encourage MVPs to stay.

Checklist to prevent the MVP from leaving

> ✓ Confirm that the person truly is an MVP and not just a good worker.
>
> ✓ Tell the MVP that he or she is truly valued by you and by the organization. Some managers choke on this idea, fearing that this admission will give an MVP a big bargaining chip to use to get more money. It is likely that the manager was incorrect in identifying

the employee as an MVP if the employee in question does use this knowledge to squeeze for more money, since true MVPs do not behave in this way. If the person does want more money, then the manager can buy the employee's presence while he or she finds and installs a successor.

✓ Make the connection. Learn about the MVP at work and outside of work. What are the MVP's challenges inside and outside the workplace? What does he or she value? How can the organization support these needs and desires? The organization's efforts do not need to be Herculean; they can be merely supportive.

✓ Provide recognition. Increase senior management visibility and access. Do not restrict access to senior management by requiring that all contact go through you. Make sure the recognition is appropriate to the MVP. For instance, an extremely introverted MVP may not want public recognition. Remember that you value and trust each other, so talk about what makes sense. Ensure that the MVP knows of all the resources that the company makes available to build commitment, to grow a career and to support personal needs.

✓ Commit your time and ideas. Continue to meet informally (lunch, coffee, travel, etc.) to talk about thoughts, ideas and opportunities.

✓ Define success in this effort as keeping the MVP committed to your business and not as keeping the MVP in a particular position for too long.

✓ Try not to counter-offer an offer from outside with money, title, etc. MVPs can be insulted by this, since they think their manager should have been aware of their needs before they became interested in an outside offer. However, after a discussion with the MVP, it may be worth asking if there is anything you can do to make them stay.

Summary

Six key themes emerge for addressing the prerequisites for successfully managing the MVP. These are:

- develop an appropriate culture to allow the MVP to be productive and motivated
- adopt a management style that allows the MVP to produce and grow
- provide career development and feedback
- provide the MVP with challenge
- allow for flexibility
- encourage the MVP to stay

CHAPTER 5

卍

How to Become an MVP

In previous chapters, we have drawn a careful portrait of the MVP. We have considered some of the MVP's key characteristics and described in detail what MVPs actually do to earn the MVP designation. The questions now arise, can you become an MVP and, if so, how? Clearly, if a person is simply born an MVP, *becoming* one is out of the question. So, the first question we must ask is, are MVPs born or made? If an MVP's talent is in any way subject to development, we can proceed to consider whether you already have what it takes to be an MVP and what you can do to become an MVP. This chapter, then, will address the following:

- Are MVPs born or made?
- Do you have what it takes to be an MVP?
- What can you do to become an MVP?

Are MVPs Born or Made?

Are MVPs born or made? Views vary, not least among managers and MVPs themselves. Bill O'Grady, Executive Vice President of Distribution and Sales at Pioneer, believes that "whatever endeavor you look at, whether it is economics, business, authors, or sportspeople, if you look at the true top 1 percent or 5 percent, in my opinion, on a scale of 1 to 10, 9 are born with it and 1 can develop it. I think you can take people and develop them to a certain point." Essentially Bill O'Grady is saying that of 1,000 people, 50 or fewer become MVPs. Of the 50 or fewer that do become MVPs, 45 come to it because of inborn talent and 5 become MVPs by developing "learned" skills. That means 5 out of 1,000 people, or 0.5 percent, can become MVPs based on development.

Barbara Bras, Director of Employee Development at Northwestern Mutual, takes a somewhat different view. She sees MVPs as "people who are able to take their gifts and abilities and leverage them in a way that consistently provides value within the company." For Bras, many may have the talent but few can make the talent work for them. Michael Cohen, President of GeneXP Biosciences, sees the questions similarly. "If you assume natural ability is a prerequisite, then the answers to the 'can you become an MVP' question become self-evident. You learn to look peripherally for opportunities to make a significant dent on value, where nobody is paying attention. So peripheral vision and personal initiative become at least as important as natural ability. Interestingly, once you begin to build a reputation as valuable, and are recognized as valuable by others, people are going to throw opportunity at you. From my personal experience, the challenge is to show up for the game, and do well."

John Humphrey, former Chairman of Forum, is less concerned with anchoring someone to their past than he is by respecting where someone came from. He prefers to put his emphasis on where someone is going. "I am philosophically opposed to the notion of 'you are what you are.' I prefer 'you will be what you want to be.' I think people are predisposed to move toward the light, and I think that the idea of 'what you want to be,' if not a bright light, is at least a burning light." He strongly supports talented people who are motivated to do the work of an MVP.

There is, really, no definitive answer to the nature or nurture question. People may have their opinions but neither expert nor layperson has yet decisively demonstrated talent's origins in either biology or environment. It seems sensible enough to think that both determinants are involved, but who really knows? What is quite clear is that talent, whatever its origins, needs to be developed. Even someone with the most brilliant natural talent is unlikely to succeed without at least a modicum of education. The authors' own experiences are based on working with talented people who want to increase their abilities and their value. Our experience leads us to believe that the "born or made" question is irrelevant. The important question is "Do you have the drive and the ability to constantly build your own value within your organization?" We realize that knowing where a person's drive and ability comes from is interesting and, at times, even useful; it is not, however, a critical factor in the development of an MVP. Given the importance of drive and ability, the two questions follow: do you have the talent it takes and how do you develop the talent you have?

Do You Have What It Takes to Become an MVP?

One of our interviewees describes two great managers. "They're both corporate MVPs, but they are 180 degrees different men. They manage differently, they conduct themselves differently and they have very different strengths. One is a charismatic leader. He has almost created a cult of personality around himself. He is a very empowering person. He makes personal speeches or writes personal notes to people that say, 'This is your business, take control of it and drive it, don't wait for someone to tell you something.' He leads by example. And he is very successful. The other manager is also very successful. He got there through his intellect, through tremendous strategy moves. He's been very strategic in what he's done with our business; he's created a very valuable business here. So, very different people, very different styles, very different methods, but both are, in my opinion, MVPs." How do you know if you have what it takes? There are no simple answers because, as the examples of these managers show, it can take different things. You need to begin by considering the primary variables: you, your job and your peers.

- consider yourself
- consider your job
- consider the views of established MVPs

Consider Yourself

What do you know about yourself? Most of the MVPs that we spoke with had a clear idea of their natural and their learned competencies, preferences, style, values and beliefs. Whenever possible, they find ways to tailor their work to fit their talents. Naomi Sutherland, VP of Operations and Strategy for Novations/J. Howard & Associates, sees her strengths helping her to define her job. "To do your best, it is to very important to know yourself and what motivates you. I have a strong sense of timing both for people personally and for the business. I am good at knowing what's right for our business today, which is why I have the strategy role. I help the senior team to think through how an idea over here might fit with this initiative over there. I can put pieces together in a way that helps us to evaluate what's right for us now and what's not right for us now." As part of his job as Chairman of the Board of Bright Horizons, Roger Brown focuses on what he does best. "I'm trying to use the standard that I shouldn't be doing anything if there is anybody else in the organization that could do it as well or better. I should do only those things that for some reason I am uniquely qualified to do." Even at the very top, MVPs use their knowledge of themselves to determine what they do best and what they need from their talented team.

To know whether you have the potential to become an MVP and to know whether you are in the right job to realize that potential, consider four questions:

- Do you have the motivation?
- Do you have the underlying talent?

- Is what you enjoy of value to your organization?
- Do you believe that you can make yourself into an MVP?

Do You Have the Motivation?

Our interviewees tell us that success and satisfaction work as good motivators, while riches and fame probably do not. Knowing whether you have what it takes requires an honest self-appraisal of your motive for wanting to be an MVP. MVPs seek challenge and they are curious. The way they work adds to the organization beyond their specific job and improves others who work with them. Curiosity and challenge motivate them to do the hard work necessary to make full use of their talents.

Motivation is a key component for MVPs, and that must be tied to plain old hard work. As John Humphrey, former Chairman of Forum, tells us, "I don't think of myself as talent. I think of myself as a hard worker. I think of myself as focused." Are you willing to put in the time and hard work necessary to become a high performer?

Do You Have the Underlying Talent?

Do you possess enough talent to be great at what you want to do? Can you perform at the highest levels? To be frank, it is difficult for any of us to do an objective assessment of ourselves. We tend to be hypercritical of our self-perceived shortcomings and overreliant on our self-perceived strengths. Talk with a trusted friend, colleague or boss. Ask him or her for a candid view of your abilities. Most yearly performance reviews are too formal; because they have to be documented, they are less than perfectly candid. MVPs take feedback, both good and bad, as *data to help them improve* and redirect their efforts. Sometimes the best medicine has a bitter taste. We need to combine our own perceptions with those of others whom we trust.

In addition to soliciting the views of others, you can also learn about your MVP potential by considering yourself in relation to what senior management looks for in an MVP. Although we have already discussed some of the MVP's key characteristics in Chapter 3, they are worth reviewing here.

1. **MVPs are motivated by intrinsic passion**. MVPs are passionate about creating value. They are forever raising the performance bar, and they like to keep score and need a scorecard to do this. Once they have achieved something, they want to do it again, but do it much better next time. True MVPs will not get discouraged when the score or results are against them; they will stay motivated and optimistic.

2. **MVPs always want to succeed and do not like to fail**. They take on a challenge with the expectation that they will succeed and, as importantly, with the willingness to do what it takes to succeed. They do not take success for granted and are aware that failure is possible. They watch for failure and use its possibility as a motivator to keep working.

3. **MVPs show moral courage**. MVPs aren't afraid to make tough decisions and take responsibility for the consequences. They are prepared to show moral courage in the face of a challenge. MVPs are often described as having integrity.

4. **MVPs are committed to the values and vision of the organization**. MVPs tend to be independent thinkers willing to raise questions and even objections when circumstances warrant. Yet they also tend to share the vision and values of the company. With their commitment to the direction of the company, MVPs have an impact far beyond the scope of their immediate responsibilities. Once these players are on the "team," a business can be built around them.

5. **MVPs enhance the organization's reputation**. MVPs bring in more business to the organization because of their reputation. We were told that clients, customers and people in similar and other industries will talk about

these players and say how good they are. "Good" refers both to the results they achieve and to their stature and presence. People will say that these people are the best people to deal with, that they are competitive while being fair, honest and open, and that they express and exemplify the values of the organization openly.

6. **MVPs earn the respect of colleagues**. For colleagues they embody the best of the organization. Others see them as consistent, trustworthy and passionate people who give themselves over completely to projects they believe in, challenge the value of doubtful projects, and always fulfill their promises.

There are numerous assessment tools and books that can guide your exploration. You can consult with your HR group for resources. You can also consult our Web site, **www.corporatemvp.com**, to learn what other readers have found to be useful and to submit your own ideas.

"Your MVP Potential" Questionnaire

We have taken the MVP attributes that our interviewees helped us to identify and have expanded them into a questionnaire that can help you to identify where you are strong and where you are weak. You can find the "Your MVP Potential" questionnaire in Appendix B.

The questionnaire comes in two forms. One form is worded so that you can enter your own scores as to your potential; the second form is worded so that you can ask the questions of others while you enter their scores. This will allow you to compare your view of your potential with the views of others.

The latest version of these forms are also available online at **www.corporatemvp.com**. Web site completion of these forms will provide you with a chart of your results.

Is What You Enjoy of Value to Your Organization?

A simple truth among MVPs is that they enjoy what they do. Enjoyment is key to maintaining superior work over an extended period of time. MVPs, therefore, must ask themselves, "Am I doing what I enjoy?" and "Is what I enjoy of value to my organization?" A great surfer can be a very valuable instructor in Hawaii or a high-and-dry curiosity in Idaho. If you are a shy linear thinker who is good at process analysis in a fast-growing sales-oriented consulting business, it is likely that you will have a hard time identifying opportunities where you can shine. Stick your head up and look around: is what you do central to the company's strategy? Learn as much as you can about your business's strategy *and* why it has been put in place. Again, most businesses have a formal strategy of some kind. Can you recognize the more informal strategies and what influences them? Do you understand the market that you are in and how it influences your business? The more you can link your good work to an organization's central reason for being, the greater your opportunity to be seen as an MVP.

Do You Believe That You Can Make Yourself into an MVP?

What do you think—can you do it? You are already on your way if you are willing and believe that you are able. Becoming an MVP is a long-term approach to work as opposed to a "get the next promotion" approach to a job. This approach combines excellent work skills and subject expertise with an enjoyment of the actual work activities. As Audra Bohannon of Novations/J. Howard & Associates puts it, it is key to reach "an alignment with your work and beliefs about what is important and meaningful to you." An example of this alignment is a friend of one of us who now does financial planning for individuals and small businesses. We first met when we were both in our early thirties and beginning to conquer our own worlds. He sold life insurance but he did not see himself as a life insurance salesman. He saw himself as a good guy in his thirties who had expertise in an important part of life that other guys in their thirties preferred to avoid—the possibility of dying. He knew that a person with a family had responsibilities that death did not erase. He saw that his job was to help others to understand the uncertain realities of the future and to manage these realities. Yes, his solution was life insurance, but his meaningful goal was to make sure that people secured their future and that of their loved ones. This may sound like a comfortable way to rationalize a moneymaking proposition but he believed in this as an important service and his sincerity showed. His long list of friends who are clients would attest to his view that he has provided them with a vital service. We are now in our fifties and the importance of what he did for his clients 20 years ago is more evident than ever. He is at the top of his profession and now teaches others his approach to the work. He is by all measures an MVP and he became an MVP by doing what he values and what he believes in.

Many of the people that we interviewed warn against pursuing MVP status as a goal. They recognize that becoming an MVP is not a goal but rather a result of attaining other meaningful work-related goals. Great movies are not made to win an Oscar but rather to reach and move an audience. The best movies are then nominated for the award. Of course, the Oscar award and other honors exist in the real world where politics and greed thrive. Smart and manipulating people may plot to "win" the award and may ultimately succeed but our interviews with MVPs made it clear that an applied veneer of MVP behavior wears thin over time. While an actor can put an Oscar statue on a shelf, an MVP renews his or her status everyday.

Consider Your Job

While it does not guarantee success, the right job can offer MVPs the opportunity to dramatically increase their value. The wrong job, however, can stifle, frustrate, diminish and disenchant even the most valuable people. Both the employer and the employee should monitor job matching. The job match should be considered by both parties when a good person begins to slide into mediocrity. The talented employee needs a hospitable organization to become an MVP. A pain-in-the-neck, never-satisfied troublemaker in one place could be a change-stimulating creative MVP in another. Both the person and the job have to fit together.

MVPs are knowledgeable about themselves and about the jobs at which they can succeed. Diane Hessan, President and CEO of Communispace, sees that "there are people who are always doing a great job. Part of that is their talent and part is that MVPs pick their own job where there is a game they know they can win." Audra Bohannon of Novations/J. Howard & Associates agrees. "You have to be in alignment. There is plenty of room for you to have your own personality, but philosophically you want to be in alignment with your organization. I remember when I was coming out of college and it was one of the last days of class and we were sitting up there, all serious, and we're going to go out there and look for a job. Our professor looked at us and said, 'Now I really want you all to think about this. When you go out and start interviewing, I want you to be just as discriminate in the company you choose to work for as they are in choosing you.' And we all looked at him as though he had two heads! We said, 'We're looking for a job! We don't have time to be assessing their values and wondering whether or not this is going to be a true fit and whether or not it's too big of a corporation.' Low and behold, that was some of the best advice he could have given us because it is important for you to feel philosophically in alignment with the company you work for."

Are you a good fit with your workplace? Bob Jeffrey, Chief Executive Officer, Worldwide, of J. Walter Thompson, recalls a former boss from his mid-twenties. "In advertising you can be recruited to work on a new project by the project leader, someone other than your direct boss. If you're young, smart, and a hard worker, your reputation is often widely known throughout your company. In one of my first jobs, I was recruited for a project by someone who asked me a great 'manager' question: 'What do you want to be in the future?' At age 24, living in Manhattan, most of my thoughts were about how I was going to pay my bills and afford to eat. I really hadn't taken the luxury to think about a career path. Since

I loved where I was working and what I was doing, I gave no thought to my answer and blurted out, 'I want to be president of this agency!' Well, the guy, who was probably all of 30, looked at me like I had tried to kill him. He put me through hell for the six months of the project. It was very clear that he was afraid that I was going to undermine him and move up into his job. He taught me a lot about what to say, and to whom. I was soon recruited by another agency, with a more challenging opportunity, where I excelled." Although the young Bob Jeffrey might have shown more wisdom in his choice of answer, he might also have taken pains to ensure that he was joining the right organization to begin with, one more inclined to respect ambition.

Megwin Finegan, also of J. Walter Thompson, acts as a "pre-MVP matchmaker." Known throughout the agency as a senior person who anticipates what is needed and who needs it, she is very skilled at foreseeing what a young person can do and who that person should meet. "I find out what it is that a good, young employee likes about the business first, and what their interests are. I make sure I know what they've been doing, so I have an understanding of what their skills and expertise are. Because I happen to be in a central place, I probably automatically start thinking that this person would be great to work with so and so. And I might not even have a particular project in mind, but I try to arrange that meeting. Exposure to other people is very important." Megwin acts as an informal guide through the JWT landscape, by creating paths through what could be a dense business environment. We have seen that MVP-hospitable businesses have both formal and informal talent development resources. Does your organization build MVP development pathways?

What causes an inhospitable environment? It can be a mismatch of skills or a bad pairing of the manager and the employee. Either way, the MVP will either fix it or will leave. Diane Hessan of Communispace talks openly about a period at a prior company when her usual MVP performance temporarily slipped. "Here I am, this person that has always done a great job, and guess what? I'm in a job that is not a fit for me. I feel like I'm just screwing up. It's not that people were telling me I was a disaster. After that, when I did have situations where I took very strong performers and put them in a job that wasn't right for them and they failed, I said, 'Let's get you out of this job. It's the job—the problem is not you.' So it was great for me to have had that experience." Irwin Heller, Managing Partner of Mintz Levin experienced the pros and the cons of matching a job to his skills and his inclinations. "I'm a better partner than I was an associate. Associates have to be very detail oriented. They really have to have section 9.034 say exactly what section 493 was supposed to have said. I'm okay at that but it's not a distinguishing characteristic. I am a very good negotiator. You do that mostly when you're a partner, so the older I got, the better lawyer I became because the skill set needed was different."

A critical piece of a hospitable environment is a person to report to that you trust and respect. A terrible boss can make a heaven into a hell. However, in an institution of higher learning, nothing can replace the value of great academic colleagues. According to Jay Keyser of MIT, "science is first and foremost a social activity, and the presence of congenial colleagues that you can work with is absolutely critical for good work." He worked for many years with Morris Halle and Noam Chomsky, renowned professors of linguistics at MIT. Chomsky is a world-famous critical thinker, who has authored many books, turning his critical eye on philosophy, linguistics, politics and other topics that he saw impacting the human condition. Jay speaks of the value of such great academic colleagues. "I was invited to give a talk at Cambridge University. Afterwards, a young lecturer at Cambridge asked me what's it like to work with Chomsky. And I said well, let me tell you a story, and I told him the story of how as a graduate student I had taken a manuscript of a review I was writing for a major linguistics journal to Morris Halle who worked with me for several months helping me refine the text. When it was finished, he said I was ready to take it to Chomsky. Chomsky made a suggestion that increased its significance by an order of magnitude. Both men gave me priceless advice. From them I learned how to write a paper in my field. The young lecturer said, 'You know, that is remark-able.' I asked why. He said, 'If I had told my mentor, who was a philosopher [I won't mention the name because it's deroga-tory, but he's a famous philosopher], if I'd gone to him and asked for help, he would have given me help on Thursday. Friday night, at dinner, he would have regaled his guests with tales of my stupidity.' And I thought, 'Oh, my God! This is what hell must be like.' I didn't tell that to him, but what I really understood was how lucky I was." A great mentor can create a wonderful MVP environment.

Know When It Is Time to Move on

A number of years ago one of us worked with an account management executive who was distraught over his being laid off after 15 years at a large company. Overwhelmed with anger and fear, he found that his decision-making skills and sense of direction were paralyzed. It emerged during our dis-cussions that Fred had been angry and fearful for 10 years. "Five years into my job I realized that I wasn't great at what I was doing and that I didn't really like it. Instead of getting up and finding a new job, I always had a reason to wait. I kept waiting and I kept getting angrier with myself. As I waited, my performance and my confidence went from good to mediocre to poor. I stopped looking for new opportunities and I found myself hiding my face, not taking on new chal-lenges. I was embarrassed by my performance. Well, the company finally found me in hiding and let me go. I wish I had quit this job 10 years ago when I wanted to leave." We wish that we could provide you with a happy ending to this story but Fred never did regain an executive-level job. Fred was a victim of *job inertia*. Work was not satisfying but it was not painful enough to encourage him to make a job change. Why risk the immediate sharp pain of making a job change when he could put up with the mild dull pain of long-term dissatisfaction? Why indeed?

Job inertia is like a cancer to MVPs. It is a slow and painful way to end a career and end up in "just a job." The way to prevent job inertia is to inoculate yourself with learning and growth.

Consider the Views of Established MVPs

Every good organization has its share of MVPs—learn from them. An important decision for any talented and ambitious person in an organization is to determine who is the best confidant and role model. You want to follow and learn from a leader who is a winner.

John Kordsmeier, Vice President of Northwestern Mutual, speaks directly to the issue of learning from others. "Many people have been important and very helpful to me for very different reasons. And sometimes it's not only because of the positive things that I learned from them, but it can be, too, from some of what they even recognize would be limitations—it can teach a lesson in itself that you don't want to go in that direction with your growth and development. So you learn both ways if you pay close enough attention. Barb Piehler and Sue Lueger [colleagues at Northwestern] have taught me about myself. What I appreciated most about Barb was her honesty when she took on the management of a complex technical department. She basically said about herself, 'Look, I don't know all the ins and outs of every process and every technicality that's involved here. But I know that I'm smart enough to learn in order to do the kind of problem solving that we need to do, and I surround myself with technically competent people who will be able to handle those areas. My job is more to steer the ship, to give guidance, to bring people along.' That was such a blinding insight to me, and was so supportive of what I think the right thing is, the right model. Sue Lueger told me that one of my deficiencies was in being direct, and being able to give feedback on a timely basis to someone that is not performing as well as they should be. She modeled it for me, and she coached me along that path, and actually, she was right. I mean, the truth is you've just got to be honest."

Sue Lueger, the Vice President of Human Resources at Northwestern Mutual, welcomes good performers who come in to think about their future. She and her department have put together a well-structured assessment and development service. "Just going through the assessment process itself makes them [top performers] think about their careers and what they really want. Because frankly some of them haven't. They just don't. Sometimes it amazes me but they really haven't thought about where they're going to be in 5 or 10 years. And yet they're still really good, so the assessment gets them to think about their own development and what they should be focusing and concentrating on."

We asked all the interviewees what they would say to a good performer asking how they could add more value to the organization. They all commented that they would welcome that type of discussion.

We have effectively rewritten the definition of success for MVPs within their organizations. MVPs routinely meet and exceed expectations, which is the typical measure of success for talented people. MVPs measure their success by *regularly increasing their value to their organization and by finding ways to increase the value of the organization to themselves.*

The next section looks at what you can do to become an MVP. It will offer lessons that we learned from MVPs and their colleagues. As you read this section we urge you to keep in mind that these recommendations do not guarantee that you will become an MVP. The following recommendations do push you to *constantly increase your value within your organization.* The more *valuable* you are within your organization, the more likely it is that you will be viewed as a *Most Valuable Performer.*

What Can You Do to Become an MVP?

In Chapter 3 we described what MVPs look like to others in the organization. We asked our interviewees, "How would you pick an MVP out of a crowd of peers?" From their answers we developed a definition of the MVP. Here is an overview of the defining MVP characteristics as seen by others:

- They focus on creating value for all stakeholders.
- They get things done.
- They are subject matter experts, either in technical or functional areas, or as general managers.
- They constantly push the envelope to make improvements.
- They represent the company well both internally and externally.
- They are great role models; they make others better.
- They are team players.
- They develop others.
- They help others succeed.
- They can get others to follow and earn the respect of others.
- They are intelligent and open-minded.

This list of how MVPs are seen by others begs the question of what a talented person can do to be seen as an MVP. The following ideas and recommendations for becoming an MVP have been developed using our interviews, our experience with MVPs, and other source data as noted. No one idea or recommendation is completely right for any particular person's profile. They are provided to offer you a composite overview of what the MVPs that we have talked with consider to be important.

If you have questions or ideas regarding your specific situation or organization that you would like to discuss, we suggest that you contact your HR department for assistance. If you desire other resources, you can check our Web site, www.corporatemvp.com.

As part of our interviews we asked, "What would you say to a talented person in your organization who came to you and asked what they could do to become an MVP?" We found the responses fell into the seven categories listed below.

To be seen as MVPs, talented people can:

1. take calculated risks
2. take advantage of luck
3. accept challenges
4. pursue meaningful work
5. engage in honest dialogue
6. recognize that attitude makes a difference
7. learn and grow

Each category covers a range of activities and behaviors, many of which overlap. For instance, it is best to take a calculated risk in the pursuit of meaningful work. As you read these category descriptions, learn each individually and understand how they fit together to create a whole approach to work.

1. Take Calculated Risks

Our interviewees had a great deal to say about the role and the value of risk-taking by people who are considered MVPs. Many MVPs are willing to take career risks—take over a failing area to turn it around, create a new product or service, move to jobs others don't want, move to other countries or try new jobs with unproven skills. As Mike Hyter of Novations/J. Howard & Associates explains, "Risk is learning, and risk-aversion is not learning."

Stan Shelton of State Street sees that "You really have to take a chance professionally. I haven't seen that many people in important roles have gotten into these roles by working their way up slowly. To really add substantial value to the company, it just seems to me that you have to be willing to take appropriate career chances. But if you never get off that first step, then you've got a problem. You could be a potentially valuable person, but if you don't have the other attributes to see and seize those opportunities, you're never going to get there."

We asked Tim Harbert, Chairman and CEO of SSgA, how he would respond to an employee's risky query on how to succeed within the firm. His responded "I would want him or her to be able to flesh that out a little bit more, to show that he or she had something in mind. Typically I would want to seek from them where they think that they can add value to the firm, rather than me telling them. That gives me a window on how broadly they think and also to affirm that it's not just a promotional exercise or a monetary financial reward exercise versus the value to the firm. But once I elicited that from them, I would say, 'Good, let's sit down with your supervisor, with your superior, and let's talk or let's have lunch or a cup of coffee and let's the three of us talk about it.' Because the worst thing I think one can do is go around the leadership team, and, as we say, dip down and pick cherries off the tree. What I look for in these encounters are people who say, 'I can do more. Glad to do more.'"

Barbara Piehler of Northwestern Mutual believes that a specific fear keeps people quiet because they are "afraid to say something that someone else would think is a dumb question. You've got to stretch yourself and you've got to be willing to put yourself out there." MVPs are willing to chance being seen as foolish.

Ed Schein of MIT Sloan School of Management recalls a study at Stanford by Tom Harrell, who followed the careers of Stanford business school alumni for 10 years. "The one personality trait that consistently correlated with overall success was social ascendancy. People were always moving forward, always pushing themselves. They preferred to be assertive rather than passive and that's probably a necessary but not sufficient characteristic of an MVP."

John Kordsmeier of Northwestern Mutual also talks of the importance of risk-taking as a manager. "I think my value for the company is that I don't manage to the middle. I manage to what I think is the right thing to do even if it causes some pain to get there. A lot of people are in the middle, and they're purposefully in the middle because they think it's the stable way to secure their future. But if, on the other hand, if you're willing to forge ahead, try new things, risk failure, then I think it will be recognized in an organization."

For Kordsmeier, however, being willing to take risks does not mean overconfidence. "I'm never really too afraid of not being competent, but occasionally the thought enters my mind. But from the feedback that I get and the challenges I know I have met, I know that it's not true, but still it's something that's back there as you talk to yourself." MVPs maintain a healthy skepticism about their invincibility. Oliver Wendell Holmes, Jr., a member of the United States Supreme Court for over 30 years, is credited with having said, "Young man, the secret of my success is that at an early age I discovered that I was not God."

Risk has no inherent value; you want to reduce it by as much as possible. Risk is simply a by-product of ambition. MVPs can reduce a problem's risk dramatically by focusing on the key variables, by creating solution options and by choosing the best option to guide their actions. MVPs create clarity in a sea of fog, thereby reducing the risk of running their ship aground.

MVPs are more risk tolerant than most, yet they worry about navigating through the fog of business as much as the rest of us. But they also have confidence in their ability to know what to do when the next problem surfaces. They fully expect that the next problem *will* surface, thereby reducing their worry about *if* it will surface. *MVPs tend to be serial problem solvers.*

2. Take Advantage of Luck

Many people may read the stories of the MVPs in this book and conclude that, yes, these are very competent people. They may also conclude that they are lucky—lucky to have had the opportunities that they have come across, lucky to work in a growing organization or for a terrific boss. In truth, almost all of the MVPs interviewed viewed themselves as lucky. However, if MVPs don't exactly manufacture their own luck, they clearly have a hand in its creation and its exploitation. They confirm Thomas Jefferson's experience, "I find that the harder I work, the more luck I seem to have."

You can work at increasing your luck when you consider it to be a combination of one part preparation and one part opportunity. The person who has prepared for an opportunity through study, experience, practice and commitment is more likely to notice an opportunity in his or her area of expertise. Thomas Edison prepared for the invention of the light bulb by learning to be an inventor, by surrounding himself with other inventors and by recognizing that electricity produces light. Then it only took him years of hard work and frustration to finally produce a viable light bulb.

It is risky waiting around for luck to strike you like a bolt of lightening. Luck is a tool of the MVP; learn to use it.

3. Accept Challenges

The acceptance of a challenge is the fuel of progress. In 1961 John F. Kennedy challenged the people of the United States to do what at the time was impossible—to put a man on the moon by the end of the decade. While he did not live to see the result, his challenge was met on July 20, 1969.

Another statement credited to Oliver Wendell Holmes, Jr. is relevant to the importance of accepting challenges: "Man's mind stretched to a new idea never goes back to its original dimensions." Accepting a challenge does not just rely on existing knowledge; it creates the opportunity for new knowledge. MVPs find the creation of knowledge to be an exciting endeavor. In our interviews we asked MVPs, senior managers and HR professionals, "What keeps an MVP happy?" We thought that we would learn about the work environment, compensation and the like. In fact, the answers are almost all similar to what John Marrs of SSgA has to say. "The challenge at work. I think they want to be intellectually stimulated and challenged." John Kordsmeier of Northwestern Mutual finds that he "gets bored easily. After two or three years in a particular job, my tendency has been to go and pursue opportunities that would present different kinds of challenges for me." John's colleague, Barbara Piehler, is very clear on the value of challenge. "I know that Northwestern considers me valuable because they keep giving me challenges. I don't like sitting back and saying, 'Why doesn't this work?' I'm going to try to fix it. That's the way I am. I like challenges. There was a gentleman that was retiring and I went to my boss at the time and said, 'I want that job. I really want that job. Never done that job before.'" Stimulation and challenge are powerful motivators for MVPs. Their work is a critical component of their lives, providing them with excitement and testing their abilities.

Challenges excite, tax and propel MVPs while improving their organizations. Challenge engages an MVP's talents with the business result of improving the organization. It links the best interests of both. The prospective MVP should actively seek challenges out.

4. Pursue Meaningful Work

It's not just a job, it's an adventure! The U.S. Navy used this now-ubiquitous phrase for years as a successful recruiting slogan. It does capture the idea that a real difference exists between working at a job and participating in an exciting experience. We found that MVPs rarely work at a job, while they do participate in an exciting experience. In Chapter 3 we said that MVPs "are motivated by intrinsic passion." It's the meaningfulness of their work that propels passion.

The work MVPs do is an integral part of their identity. Their work is an important component of the way they interact with their world. They know what they value and what they believe in, and work is aligned with these values and beliefs. Audra Bohannon, Senior Vice President, Product Development at Novations/J. Howard & Associates, expressed this alignment this way: "I'm saying work is wonderful when both you and the organization win. I am a big proponent of 'it is not right for the organization to win and you lose and it is not right for you to win and the organization lose.' It is really important for both of your agendas to be integrated in a way that you feel that you have benefited and the organization feels like it has benefited."

A strong theme throughout the interviews is "work is meaningful" in a very personal way for MVPs. The words, passion, love, commitment, excitement, enjoyment and fun are frequently used to explain an MVP's reasons for their risk-taking, long hours and great effort. Audra Bohannon is a prime example of someone whose work is meaningful. "And the reason why [I have been successful] is because I'm so *passionate* about my work. So, every time I get a group that walks in the [training] room, I'm ready to go." One reason that Keith Brown of FiRE + iCE restaurants is excited about his work was because following our book interview he was flying out to Lake Tahoe to open a new restaurant. He explains his excitement this way: "Jim [the Chairman] and I have been working on this opening [of a new restaurant] for a long time. It really takes us national. It is very exciting. I don't know how you get people to be excited and passionate about their work because some of them have it and some of them don't. I really think a lot of it comes down to a sense of ownership and how much autonomy they have in their work." Barbara Piehler of Northwestern Mutual is very clear about what work means to her and how it is aligned with what she *loves*. "I love working with people, I love getting people to do what they do best. I work best through people and I like challenges."

John Hatsopoulos of *American*DG sees the strong personal connection to work when it offers the person *independence.* "You know it's interesting, I meet lots of people when I am in New York City, and because some of them happen to be Greek I end up talking to them. I asked guys why they drive a taxi, when they could make a hell of a lot more money working by the hour. And they say, 'Because it's my own business.' How many hours do they work? 'Oh, 14 a day, 7 days a week. But it's my business. Nobody tells me what to do.' They either make it or they don't make it. That's right! They say, 'I'm saving money and buying my own [Eagle] Medallion and it is worth $X and along the way I'll maybe buy another taxi.' So they kill themselves for rides. People love it. And these are people who want to work. They are passionate and intelligent."

John Kordsmeier of Northwestern Mutual left teaching theology over 20 years ago to join his company. He recalls his decision this way: "To be honest it was the most difficult decision of my life, because I was passionate about teaching. One of the reasons I like this company is that outside of the work that I do here on a daily basis, I still have the opportunity in my personal life to teach and work with youth. And it's the fact that this *freedom* can allow me to walk away from here and continue to be involved in the community that makes me more energized to do the work I need to do here as well." He knows that he could leave Northwestern Mutual and be fulfilled teaching. This knowledge gives him a sense of freedom that allows him to take career risks that others may avoid to maintain a secure position.

Stan Shelton of State Street speaks of the meaning of work for MVPs. "I think it's a common trait. These individuals believe in what they're doing, what we're doing as an organization. And they see their role as being an important part of the whole. And again it's a natural extension of the confident and *optimistic* approach that they have in their lives. So they're not working as much as they are being in their careers. It's not a chore for them to come in every day and do the parts of their role that they're actually very good at. I believe that the individuals I'm thinking of are inspired by the opportunities that we as a group feel we have."

Our interviewees had much to say about the meaning of work. They spoke of *passion and love, commitment, independence and freedom, and an optimistic belief in opportunities*. Here are some other thoughts on meaningful work:

Balance: Daniel Behr of Seed Partners says, "These people are smart in what they do. In terms of balancing things, they think about it. They like their work. They are happy at work and they make sure that they're happy at home."

Trust and Respect: Daniel Behr says, "Trusted and respected, to me that's it. There should be an excitement about going to an MVP with an idea. There should be no hesitation to go to the MVP and say, you know, we [the investors] don't like this, here's why. Because if it's treated with respect, within the context of information, then what do you have to fear?"

Crystal-Clear Vision: John Kordsmeier of Northwestern Mutual feels that "The brand here is crystal clear in people's minds. And we're about long-term value for our policy owners. That becomes part of the fabric here, and it becomes so inculcated that you don't have to worry about people not understanding what we are about. And it's precisely that which forms, in a way, a religion of its own. Or it's at least a passionate commitment to what the company's about that keeps you engaged. So it's really not dissimilar from the theology career."

Satisfaction: Stan Shelton of State Street states, "The role I play, I get a lot of satisfaction out of it, and it comes relatively naturally to me. I think that's kind of an important point—it's not asking MVPs to step outside of their natural inclinations, how they want to work and interact with others."

Responsibility: Jim Miller of FiRE + iCE says, "I find an MVP is someone whose reliability and talent are almost interchangeable. If people simply do what they say they will do, that immediately distinguishes them in my mind. I don't mean that in an unthinking, follow-the-rules sense, but in a responsible sense. If someone tells me something is going to be done on Friday at 3:00 and it is done at 3:00 on Friday, I know I've got a special talent. They don't give me any reasons why it isn't done, they don't brag to me that it was done—they simply do it. That is the beginning of trust and that trust is the beginning of acknowledging extraordinary talent. It leads to greater and greater responsibility on their part, and reliance on mine."

5. Engage in Honest Dialogue

Barbara Bras, Northwestern Mutual, Director of Employee Development spoke about what Northwestern does to develop MVPs and what the MVPs do to constantly increase their values, "This is what we see works for MVPs. It's taking who they are as unique individuals and then leveraging that into the highest and best use in the organization. When I look at

MVPs, I think that they are people who seek out and get feedback and then use it. I think they're also people who don't dwell on their weaknesses; they capitalize on their strengths."

The bedrock of integrity and trust is open and honest communication. If you hear only good things about yourself from your colleagues and then you find out about something bad, you naturally wonder why you hadn't heard of these problems before. Truthful people give honest opinions. Gerry Lupacchino of Novations/J. Howard & Associates talks about open and honest communications as a basic work skill and as an expectation of each other. "We give each other feedback a lot. I ask for it all the time and they ask for it as well."

When talking of honest communication with our interviewees we often heard that "transparency" is important. We wondered how "transparent" or easily understood the term itself is. Tim Harbert, Chairman and CEO of SSgA, defines what it means to him. "Transparency means that the person is comfortable in getting and understanding all the facts, searching for the facts, searching for the truth, if you will, and then going ahead and making decisions and then communicating clearly why that decision was made and what the key attributes were in that decision. In other words, you can see right through their thought process, with nothing to hide."

Ned Walker, Senior Vice President, Worldwide Corporate Communications, Continental Airlines, remembers how Continental had had a string of CEOs before Gordon Bethune took over and how one of the results was that employees had lost faith and trust in senior management. "It was clear to me [when Gordon Bethune took over Continental Airlines] that we were going to be successful, because he had the drive. He had the leadership skills. He had the charisma. And he was willing to say the tough things that needed to be told to the employees. We needed to do some cuts right up front and we went out and had some employee meetings and told employees some things that were tough, you know, that we needed to cut some of our workforce; we needed to cut back; we needed to get rid of some of our airplanes. And it wasn't a popular message, but Gordon basically said, 'Whether it's popular or not, I really don't care. Here's what we need to do.' And, I think, then employees began to understand that Gordon is totally candid, and the management team here is totally candid. His marching orders were 'we'll tell the employees everything we can tell them, whether it's good or whether it's bad.'" It worked for Continental. After more than 10 years of steady leadership that emphasizes honest communication and lots of hard work by all employees, it is now one of the world's best airlines and one of *Fortune* magazine's "Best Companies to Work for."

6. Recognize That Attitude Makes a Difference

MVPs believe that they will succeed. They also know that they will meet obstacles along the way to success and they believe that they will be able to overcome those obstacles. Martin Seligman, the author of *Learned Optimism*, has done extensive research on the power of attitude. He draws a clear distinction between pessimists and optimists. "The defining characteristic of pessimists is that they tend to believe bad events will last for a long time, will undermine everything they do, and are their own fault. The optimists, who are confronted with the same hard knocks of this world, think about misfortune in the opposite way. They tend to believe defeat is a temporary setback, that its causes are confined to this one case. Confronted by a bad situation, they perceive it as a challenge and try harder."[1]

MVPs tend to have a positive attitude. According to Seligman, optimists live longer and succeed more often, while pessimists suffer more illness and give up in failure more often. The question of what you can do to become an MVP includes what you can do to become an optimist. Seligman's answer is that "becoming an optimist depends not on mindless devices like whistling a happy tune or mouthing platitudes ("Every day in every way, I'm getting better and better"), but on "learning a new set of cognitive skills."[2]

---

[1] Martin A. Seligman, *Learned Optimism* (New York: The Free Press, 1998), 4–5.

[2] Ibid.

Seligman looks at the traditional psychological view of achievement as a combination of talent and desire. He asks, "What if there is a third factor—optimism or pessimism—that matters as much as talent or desire?"[3] We found that this factor definitely influences the way other people perceive MVPs. A great performer with a pessimistic attitude is appreciated for his or her performance but does not have that *plus* factor expected of an MVP. We can only wonder what pessimistic great performers could achieve if they were not burdened by the weight of their debilitating tendencies. We recommend Seligman's book to anyone who feels less than optimistic or who feels downright pessimistic or depressed, and who wants to learn optimism.

Confirming Seligman's emphasis on optimism, several of our interviewees comment on the power of having a good attitude. Naomi Sutherland of Novations/J. Howard & Associates is representative. She observes, "MVPs have so much to do with mindset. If you are a person who sees obstacles as problems, you're going to be a person who wants to do the minimum; it's not going to happen.... I haven't met any MVPs that are sour or negative and I think sort of by default the best people tend to be personable, they are able to express themselves, they are able to do what they said they would do, they are able to generate resources. So if they have an idea, they are not limited by the fact that they can't implement it. They are able to generate some interest and excitement about it. I think you have to be in that positive, problem-solving, 'see things that haven't been seen before' mindset to truly be most valuable." Bill O'Grady of Pioneer talks of attitude. He believes that "If you look at real MVPs, first of all they have the skill to do their job. They also bring their personal impact and power but so much of it is motivation—*it's the old, you really oughta wanna!* Some people can get motivated for a day or a week or a month, but to be able to do it for years and decades, that I think is innate." *Desire* pushes many people through many obstacles.

---

[3] Martin A. Seligman, *Learned Optimism* (New York: The Free Press, 1998), 4–5.

Tim Harbert of SSgA talks about who he values and why. "What I look for as the most valuable performer are individuals who are excellent intellectually and in their work, and also in their personality. I look for characteristics that point to open communication, transparency, integrity, decision-making ability, consensus building. I like a player-coach, in other words; they can do the job and they can also coach people, supervise them, mentor them in jobs. They have often come up through the ranks, succeeding as a member of the team. They don't carry an attitude with them: 'I have X years experience, so this task that needs doing is too lowly for me.' They expect to work as a team and to do what is required."

Attitudes can be innate; they can also be learned from people of importance to us. Audra Bohannon of Novations/J. Howard & Associates is valued for many things, including always being ready to help out her colleagues. She traces her willingness to *volunteer* back to her early influences. "I think there is something that made a huge difference in my life, and I didn't realize it until just two weeks ago when my grandmother passed. She would have been 86 in July. I had to put her obituary together and it allowed me to really.... I had to call friends and family to pull all this information together. In doing this, I had the chance to really understand what a wonderful grandmother she was and what her life was like before I came into this world. She founded and was a member of five different organizations in our small city. She was a beautician and a pioneer in the field of cosmetology. She was very much about service and I never understood the degree to which she had such a passion for service until I saw it all written in black and white. Now I understood where I got my value for service, for volunteering, for being there for others—from my grandmother. From a very early time, I always volunteered. When I was 13 years old I was a volunteer at Head Start and when I was 14 they brought me back as an employee. I would always raise my hand first. Didn't know how I was going to do it, but I was always willing. And quite often, I would be asked back as an employee. And even today, I am of service and I am willing to give my time to volunteer and I usually get asked to come back."

John Humphrey, formerly of Forum, expands the typical understanding of volunteering. "Remember when we had the problems with the Japanese and their quality circles? The Japanese described them as voluntary. We tried that and it didn't work. I went to Japan and found they are voluntary but not discretionary. I learned that voluntary means "with a willing spirit." So I realized that all the people in my organization were volunteers. They were all recruited once a quarter. They were all free agents. The contract we had with them was about the importance and meaningfulness of the work and their personal growth. These people were volunteers in the Japanese sense of the word. They work with a *willing spirit.*" MVPs are optimists who work with a willing spirit and who choose to come to work everyday.

One additional observation on MVPs' attitudes: they are not pumped up with *self-importance* and have little tolerance for it. According to Gordon Bethune, Chairman and CEO of Continental Airlines, "You've got to get that lesson early. Self-importance can ruin it for a lot of people. It gets in the way of a lot of stuff and it doesn't give anybody a sense of belonging. Nobody wants to say, 'I'm not as good as you are.' You're not making anybody feel good about that. First of all it's not true. Do your job well and you'll get plenty of recognition. I get more than I deserve. I just get it. When I get asked to give a speech, it isn't because Gordon Bethune's a great guy. He represents a bunch a people who have done a wonderful job and got national recognition and I just happened to epitomize the name, but I didn't do it." Mike Campbell of Continental Airlines agrees, "There is a question of managing talented people that's separate from MVPs. I think the real issue there is around their believing their own press. The thing you often hear about these people is they don't relate well. They usually don't think they have peers in terms of intellect and people who contribute to the company, and they become in many cases those talented people who don't become MVPs—it's because of their people relationships; they usually don't see their own limitations. They think their brilliance is everything and more."

7. Learn and Grow

Simon Wilson-Taylor, Managing Director and Senior Vice President of Global Link at State Street, tells us that from childhood he never "really had any doubt that [he] would be successful." He also knew that he, like everyone else, had his personal challenges to overcome. "Shyness got to me until well into adulthood. Well, to the extent that even in my mid- to late twenties it was difficult for me to enter into conversation in a group of more than two people without feeling embarrassed and awkward about it. And the only way to address that was to attack it head on. I accomplished that by taking on a job that required me to be a salesperson and a public speaker. That's effectively what I did for most of that time in my twenties." We would not describe Simon as shy today.

Get up out of your desk chair and stretch those mental muscles every so often. Muscles and minds that are not exercised atrophy and stiffen. Active learners are the seed group from which MVPs sprout. An executive tells us that he always knew where to look for MVPs. "There is a group of people who learn and who are observant enough to be able to figure out what they do correctly and what they do incorrectly. That is the group from which I find MVPs. I'm sure there's some with God-given talent, but as far as becoming an MVP, they have to be aware of what the MVP does and be flexible enough to fit into the description. I would say for the most part, they are made." MVPs are made by learning. Books, trainings and classes can provide excellent ways to learn. So can experience.

Learning needed skills is sometimes a matter of finding a job or project in which those skills must be developed. Lou de Ocejo, the Executive Vice President of Human Resources for State Street, knows that a business must invest in developing its best people. "A lot of companies talk about development. They talk about it even if they haven't reviewed it with their people, and they do little about it! By the way, everybody thinks it's an event-driven thing, which is usually not the best development. The best personal development I ever had in my career was work! I went to work somewhere where I didn't know much, but I had to learn it. People were willing to teach me and I became productive. Then when I got productive enough to be dangerous, I got yanked out and went somewhere else where I could be unproductive for another period of time to learn something new and different. School is wonderful, it's great, but it's a poor substitute for experience. Experience is best in real time. Experience isn't fake."

A key element of learning on the job is simply listening. At Northwestern Mutual, John Kordsmeier has taken on a series of challenging assignments where the company has identified a need for change. These assignments usually last three years or longer. John is known to be a pretty smart guy who prepares himself well prior to stepping into a new role. Here is how John begins to work with a new group in need of some change, some updating, some improvement: "Even if I have an idea about what needs to be done, I'm going to go in there and resist my preconceived views. I spend a good part of my time just listening and finding out what's going on. And then, I can act in an informed way. I spend my first six or eight months talking to the people who are doing the work within the group, getting their own perspective, and then find out where the gaps are and start building towards filling those gaps. That's in general the approach. By listening you really overcome some of the prejudices that you may enter into a position with, and we all do have our own prejudices." John would prefer to learn from others, more than impress others. Why take chances, he wonders, when you can learn from the experts?

Observing how established MVPs perform is also essential to learning. Yet, as Nick Bonn of State Street warns, there is no one path to success. You have to discover what works for you. "I've watched a number of different people in my career, successful people, and tried to see how they do it. And it's clear that there's no pretty, plain and straightforward way to do it, no one personality type that ensures success, and no one method. I've watched some of these people, and tried to learn from them. And certainly I can never be a leader the way some of those guys are, but I do recognize in my own way I have to be a leader to the 100 people that I manage, as well as the 500 people in my division that I don't manage but I'm supposed to influence."

Inevitably, learning from experience and learning from others involve facing up to your weaknesses and inadequacies. For Barbara Bras of Northwestern Mutual, it's important to use that confrontation positively. "When I look at MVPs, I think that they are people who get and use feedback, but I think they're also people who don't dwell on their weaknesses. They acknowledge their areas of weakness and they find ways to succeed by filling in those gaps or by increasing their strength. What they do not do is deny that weakness and basically create a hole for themselves at work to fall in." MVPs identify the weaknesses as part of the process of eliminating them.

Audra Bohannon's views are representative. "Do not commit to things that you cannot deliver. Recognize that your time and energy has limits. Saying no to a commitment in an explanatory manner that the other person can understand is better than disappointing that person when you do not meet the commitment. That includes knowing why you may have to say no to yourself. You've got to do the cost/benefit analysis. If you are going to go back to school to get your MBA, it's going to impact your time with your family. So, how are you going to manage it? When I make a decision that I'm going to go for it I weigh both how I will benefit and what the cost will be."

Learning and growing are fed by everyday experience and by planned activities. Both have value. To truly integrate this learning you can ask yourself these four simple questions that we see promotes *efficient learning*:

1. **What did I just learn?** Be aware of the times you experience something that could be considered learning. When you recognize such a time, it is important to review it, to "say" it to yourself. This forces you to be aware of what you just learned and to synthesize it from just a memory into an idea that you can store and relate to other ideas.

2. **How does this idea apply to my situation?** Take your idea and link it to a recent or current situation or

problem. This link will allow you to remember the idea when you face a similar situation or problem.

3. **What other ideas that I hold are challenged by this idea?** This question will force you to confront conflicting ideas, each of which you may have reasons to defend. Better to recognize this conflict now rather than in the middle of action. You can also determine which ideas should be kept, modified or thrown out.

4. **Does this new idea stimulate other learning opportunities?** Always look for your next challenge.

When many of our interviewees spoke of MVPs as open and flexible they were talking about a person's openness for learning and his or her flexibility for growing.

꿘

How, then, do you become an MVP? Let's end with some advice from John Humphrey of Forum. "I would say, spend a lot of time looking at people, and trying things out, and testing things out, and put yourself in positions where you will be tested. Create obligations for yourself that will drag you into performing situations and then seek feedback. The next thing I would say is find a mentor or mentors. Choose that mentor carefully. You've got to find a mentor who is in that event. If you have the right event and you have someone interested in you, it's mostly a matter of chemistry. Mentor is a temporary position. Overlong mentorships end badly. Then find and use ways that will give you the opportunity to build and demonstrate those skills. What's the old saying—'Many are able, few are chosen.' So play in the street. One of the clearest things I would say to people is to use failure as an opportunity to grow rather than to limit your activities."

Talent is important, but it is not everything. Drive and the requisite skills are also essential. It is up to you to decide how much you want to be the best of the best.

Summary

This chapter explored the important question of whether or not people can make themselves into MVPs. Four areas were covered:

- Each MVP is a unique blend of natural talent and learned excellence.

- Not everyone has the ability and/or the desire to become an MVP.

- People who are deemed to be MVPs are so chosen because of how their work and their organizational participation is perceived by influential people within that organization.

- People who do have the ability and the desire to become an MVP can learn what is important to do from other MVPs. This includes:

  1. taking calculated risks

  2. taking advantage of luck

  3. accepting challenges

  4. pursuing meaningful work

  5. engaging in honest dialogue

  6. recognizing that attitude makes a difference

  7. learning and growing

- MVPs measure their success by regularly increasing their value to their organization and by finding ways to increase the value of the organization to themselves.

Suggested Resources

1. Martin A. Seligman, *Learned Optimism* (New York: The Free Press, 1998).

CHAPTER 6

卍

Bringing in the MVP
from Outside

First, a cautionary tale. A company with a seriously under-performing customer care services department recruited an external candidate, in fact an MVP, from a similar organization to take on the job of turning the department around. The department had been losing customers for four years and had failed to respond to all previous attempts at remediation. The new manager, our MVP, was given the eight months before the beginning of the company's next busy season to effect a fix. At least two obstacles stood in his way: many of his sometimes underperforming staff had highly specialized skills and could not be easily replaced; and his immediate boss, who had also been recently recruited, had a simple three-part philosophy: "Just do it, don't bother me and I don't want to hear of any problems." This boss was also somewhat intimidated by the MVP's clarity and successes. In any event, our MVP succeeded admirably. Having achieved turnarounds at two similar organizations, he knew exactly how to create a new department that delivered excellent customer service. Everyone in the company was very pleased with his results.

Unfortunately, our sad story doesn't end here. Things began to unravel when after twelve months of good performance senior management decided to change the compensation design of this department. Because the department was now performing well, it was thought appropriate to bring in a different form of compensation—and in a very short time. While the intent of the new compensation was admirable, our MVP was not given time to introduce it in a way that would be acceptable to his department. Told just to fix it, he complained bitterly to senior management, but to no avail. In fact, his "obstinacy" undermined management's confidence in him and he was soon asked to leave. In the aftermath, the MVP was happily reunited with his former organization and the department he had worked so hard to turn around reverted to its customary poor performance.

So what went wrong? Clearly the organization thought that it was bringing in a person who could fix the problems of the department, and indeed he did fix those problems. Why did the MVP not succeed in his new organization? The reasons were several:

- The MVP had not completely clarified the expectations of senior management on an ongoing basis, and was totally unprepared for the change in compensation. While he may have known what was expected of him when he joined the company, he did not keep up to date with the changing expectations that he was required to meet.

- His direct manager had no interest in working with him to address the broader organizational issues and was unable to help him navigate the cultural realities of the organization, since he himself was new to the organization. This manager highlighted the MVP's problems to set him up as a scapegoat for the manager's own deficiencies.

- His behavior was probably at odds with that of other managers and he was not given the feedback on how to influence change in the organization. His challenging of the cultural norms felt threatening to incumbent managers in other areas.

- He had not built strong relationships with the existing and long tenured managers in the organization who could have guided him through the intricacies of the organization's culture and what it took to be successful there.

This type of failure is not uncommon. Sufficient thought and planning needs to be put into the hiring and assimilation of the MVP if he or she is to thrive in the new organization.

This chapter will look at how to succeed at bringing in an MVP. It will cover the following topics:

- the reasons why externally recruited MVPs may fail
- optimizing the selection process
- optimizing the assimilation process

The Reasons Why Externally Recruited MVPs May Fail

Failure is not unusual when senior people are brought into a new organization. Research conducted by Manchester-MPS Group shows that "fully 40% of all newly appointed leaders fail to meet the expectations of their organizations."[1] In "CEO Succession 2002: Deliver or Depart," management and technology consulting firm Booz Allen Hamilton describes a typical pattern of rise and fall among senior recruits. "Outsiders excel early, outperforming insiders by nearly 7 percentage points in the first half of their tenures. In the 'second semester,' when most CEOs endure a slump, outsiders underperform insiders by 5.5%, thus failing to live up to their early promises. Outsider CEOs are at greater risk of being fired than insiders."[2] We make the assumption that both externally recruited CEOs and MVPs share similar characteristics and experiences. This section will look at:

- steps in the selection process that cause MVPs to fail
- why MVPs fail once they are in their new positions

What Steps in the Selection Process Cause MVPs to Fail?

A flawed selection process can be a root cause of MVP failure. The flaws can be various:

---

[1] Manchester-MPS Group, "New Leader Coaching," *Manchester Professional Development Solutions*, 14.

[2] Chuck Lucier, Rob Schuyt and Eric Spiegel, Booz Allen Hamilton Inc., "CEO Succession 2002: Deliver or Depart," *strategy+business Special Summer Report 2003*.

- The MVP may be interviewing for the wrong job with the wrong manager.

- Recruiters may be unclear about their expectations or the MVP's competencies.

- Recruiters may not properly communicate expected results and behaviors.

- The MVP may be blind to, or not honest about, his or her deficiencies. The individual may not fit in with the culture of the new organization.

- There may be a significant difference in values between the organization and the MVP, or the MVP and his or her manager.

The Wrong Job with the Wrong Manager

The fit between the job or the manager and the candidate may not have been properly assessed. Larry Kellner, President and COO of Continental Airlines, says that once the person has been recruited, you have to make sure that he or she is put in the right job with the right tools to do the job. "It's more about getting the right talent into the right place, and then it's about personality fit. The need for personality fit with the manager and the team is why so many people end up getting fired in one job, then go to another job and become a huge success. It's not that they were lacking in talent or that they weren't a peak performer, but that they were put in an environment where they weren't allowed to excel. Also, they weren't given a chance to express their opinions and given a chance to make things better."

**Ensuring the MVP Is Put in the
Right Place and Allowed to Excel**

The responsibility for ensuring that the MVP is in the right environment rests with both the MVP and the hiring organization. There can never be a 100 percent guarantee that the fit between the individual and the company will work, but there are ways to find out whether this will be a successful place to work.

MVPs need to:

✓ Do a thorough check of the culture of the company to see if they will fit. They also need to get some feedback on the manager they will work for. They can do this by asking for information from friends and colleagues who work at the company, or from suppliers and vendors who work with the company.

✓ Try and talk to someone who has worked for the potential manager and see what makes the manager tick and what he or she values. Find out the type of person who is a good personality fit with this manager, and who is a poor fit. This information will help the individual decide if this will be a good place to work. They have to be honest with themselves about the potential fit with the manager.

✓ Talk to recruiting firms who usually have a read on the culture of most companies and who will or won't fit.

✓ During the course of the interview, ask everyone what results the new person is expected to achieve. Then MVPs need to be honest with themselves as to whether they can achieve these results.

Managers need to:

✓ Check or have references checked to thoroughly find out what management style the person is used to, what he or she values and the type of results that the candidate has achieved in the past.

✓ Find out situations where the MVP has excelled and where he or she has not done so well.

✓ During the course of the interview process, really think through whether they can work with this person. Will the person fit well? Will he or she produce the value that is expected?

A thorough assessment of potential fit between the manager, the organization and the MVP can prevent potential hiring mistakes from happening in the future.

Improperly Assessed Expectations or Competencies

The people in the organization may not be totally clear about the skills, knowledge and experience that they desire the person to bring to the new position. They may have a general sense of what is required, but may not have a clear idea of what results they expect from the MVP and of what previous experience the MVP needs to have to deliver those results. If the organization is confused, successfully recruiting a person to meet its expectations is difficult. Remember the story of Alice who asks the Cheshire Cat for directions? The Cat replies, "That depends a good deal on where you want to get to." When Alice says she doesn't "much care where," the Cat concludes, "Then it doesn't matter which way you go." If an organization is unclear about what it wants and where it wants to go, it does not matter who is recruited, until of course the wrong person is selected and the required results do not materialize!

Improperly Communicated Expectations

Sometimes the problem boils down to miscommunication during the interview itself. Interviewers may know exactly what they want from a candidate but may not take sufficient care in, or be sufficiently open about, expressing their expectations. Equally, the MVP may misinterpret what is being said in the course of the interviews. Such miscommunication often results in MVPs failing to achieve the results or engage in the behaviors required of them. In short, they fail.

Unacknowledged Deficiencies

Another reason for failure is that MVPs may not be totally honest about their deficiencies, or even be aware of what they are.

By deficiencies we mean those things that the MVP may not do well and that can cause them to fail in the organization. If they work with their HR department and with coaches, they will be able to identify potential deficiencies and work on strategies to correct them.

Not Fitting In

During interviews, the organization may not be totally clear about describing its culture and the type of person who would fit into this culture. As a colleague of ours notes, "I think it's hard to recruit an MVP. The person who is an MVP in Company X may not be an MVP in Company Y. The thing that may have made them an MVP in Company X might be the very thing that makes them fail in Company Y. You might be mesmerized by a person's track record and not think enough about what it's going to take to be successful in a particular company. The difference in culture can mean that things are done in a very different way."

Jerry Bliley, the Vice Chairman of Spencer Stuart Canada, explains how important it is for him and the organization to clearly define the culture when hiring an MVP. "As a recruiter I need to understand the organization and its culture and the organization's desired direction, as well as understanding the individual. I think I only do half of the job if I get a really great read on the person. As a recruiter, I think it's my responsibility to understand both. When I've missed over the years, I think it's more often because I failed to understand the client organization rather than failing to understand the candidate."

Some organizations underestimate the need to take culture into consideration during recruitment. As Bliley relates, "Interestingly enough, we'll run into clients who think all of that understanding of the culture that we're trying to get upfront is something that should be self-evident and they don't want to spend time on it. Those same clients have more turnover in their organizations than they need to have. They don't understand that different organizations have different cultures and succeed in different ways."

Differences in Values

During the course of our consulting work, we have learned that one key reason MVPs fail or do not stay with an organization is that they and the organization hold different values. Sometimes those differences can be harmless, as in the case of an MVP CEO we know who was hired by an international firm to run its U.S. subsidiary. Although he exceeded expectations set for him, he ended up leaving because he did not have the autonomy to run all aspects of the organization. Autonomy was what he really valued!

In other instances, the differences involve issues of basic integrity, as in the case of a highly talented woman we know who was hired to drive the change agenda and increase efficiency in a certain company department. She had a strong change-management and development background, and high integrity. Once recruited, however, she discovered that her role was that of a spy, to provide the leader with information that would allow him to fire his senior management team! This was definitely not consistent with her values. She soon found an opportunity to leave the company for another that better suited her ethical viewpoint. The selection process may well lead to failure if MVPs and the organization do not explore their respective values openly.

Why Do MVPs Fail Once in Their New Position?

MVP failures can occur even when the selection process is by all reasonable measures successful. Once installed in the new position, the MVP may face circumstances unanticipated during recruitment:

- Expectations have changed, and the MVP is not aware of this.
- The timing for delivering required results has changed.
- The MVP fails to build strong relationships with key stakeholders.
- An internal person who did not get the job derails the MVP.

Changed Expectations

For a variety of reasons, the pace of organizational life has increased rapidly over the last few years. This increased pace, coupled with cutbacks in staff levels required to reduce operating expenses, has often meant that managers have little time to deal with the ongoing management requirements, particularly the development needs of their direct reports.

In such circumstances, managers may not inform the MVP of changes in priorities and/or the time frame in which the priorities have to be met. While the MVP may have been very clear on what was expected of him when he joined the organization, he may have been so busy trying to meet these expectations that he may not have realized that priorities or time frames had changed. Perhaps the MVP had been told by his manager to focus on increasing sales in one part of the business and did so effectively. However, he was expected to both increase sales and reduce costs.

Changed Timing

Another potential reason for failure is that although the MVP is achieving the results that have been mapped out, he is not aware that the time frame for delivering the results has been reduced. We know of a person brought into an organization to lead a very significant business in the financial services industry. The business was underperforming and required a significant turnaround. Given 18 months to achieve results, the MVP began to implement a significant number of changes and initiatives that had been approved by senior management. However, the economy and the market in which the company operated deteriorated rapidly, and the MVP was suddenly expected to turn the business around within nine months. Not having been told directly that the time frame had changed and that his planning horizon was no longer acceptable, he failed to meet expectations and was fired. This example supports the findings mentioned in the Booz Allen Hamilton report on CEO failure cited at the beginning of this chapter.

Failing to Build Relationships

It is particularly important for MVPs to build relationships with key stakeholders, and by stakeholder we mean anyone who has a stake in the work or the outcome of the work that is being performed by MVPs. This is especially true for newly recruited MVPs since stakeholders can play an essential role in passing on detailed knowledge about the political realities and culture of the organization. If MVPs fail to identify the key stakeholders and manage their expectations on an ongoing basis, they may make a number of cultural mistakes and underperform.

Yet MVPs are usually required to "hit the deck running" and start to produce results immediately. How do they make time for the analysis of who stakeholders are and how to manage their expectations when they are so busy producing results? The simple answer is that they have to make time! They can get help in doing this from such sources as their managers, their peers and their HR department. They can also make sure that they have a mentor that has been around the organization for a long time and knows what is expected and how things are done in the organization. A number of organizations engage an external coach to help MVPs get on board with what they are expected to achieve, and how to work within the culture and politics of the organization. A key piece of advice for the MVP: remember that you are hired by your manager, but promoted by your peers. These peers are often the key stakeholders in any organization.

Being Derailed

It is important for the MVP to discover early on if there were internal candidates for the position, and then to try to create a relationship with them. These people may be upset that they did not get the job. They may feel that they have the competencies required to get the job done. If the MVP does not handle these people well, they may set out to undermine the MVP, subtly doing everything they can to place the MVP in a bad light. Since they usually know who the key stakeholders and influential people in the organization are, they can begin to undermine the MVP immediately. MVPs must do what they can to gain acceptance among disappointed candidates.

Of course, in such situations, management also bears a special responsibility. As Ian Hendry of RBC Capital Markets tells us, "The fact is that when you make the big-league signing, it's possible you have climbed over solid contributors who wanted that job and didn't get it. You run the risk of derailment since those passed over can make life really hard for the new incoming executive, so deploying the talent astutely and providing the support mechanisms to improve the odds of success does become somewhat pivotal. There's an irony here for HR when we spend money on executive search and then we do little to transition them effectively."

Optimizing the Selection Process

MVPs fail because of mistakes made during the process of selection and the process of assimilation. How can organizations attract and retain MVPs successfully? What steps must be taken to ensure the long-term success of externally recruited MVPs? The answer must begin with optimizing selection. Topics covered in this section will include:

- the need to bring in an MVP
- creating the job and person description
- sources of candidates
- the interview process
- the reference check
- doing whatever it takes to ensure that the MVP joins the organization

The Need to Bring in an MVP

Most organizations prefer to hire internally. Andrew Faas, Executive Vice President of Corporate Development and Human Resources for Shoppers Drug Mart, expresses the view that was representative of many of the people that we inter-viewed: "Our model is to recruit from inside as much as possible." Yet Faas also acknowledges that "It's always healthy to have new blood brought into the organization." There are, in fact, a number of specific reasons why an organization may consider recruiting MVPs from the outside:

- It may lack critical skills necessary to meeting current and future business needs.

- It may need "new blood" to take a new approach to doing things.

- It may require new skills as it enters a new stage of growth; for example, it may be a small company rapidly becoming a large one or a single market producer on the brink of developing multiple markets.

- It may require someone with the expertise and reputation to help with the implementation phase of a critical project or the introduction of a new product or service.

- It may need a turnaround specialist to implement a dra-matic change of direction in order to improve its effectiveness.

- It may need to restock its talent pool to ensure the avail-ability of suitable successors when key positions fall vacant.

As well as having very specific reasons for hiring external-ly, many organizations also often have the broader picture in mind. "When we do hire somebody from outside," Faas tells us, "we don't hire just to fill for the role, but with the view to having that person progress long term." Dan Geraci, President and CEO of Phoenix Investment Partners, explains that he is constantly on the lookout for talented people in order to meet future as well as current business needs. "You need to introduce fresh ideas, fresh blood, fresh DNA into the gene pool of the firm all the time, and so you go out and try to find a person who has a combination of the current skills needed and the future potential for growth so that what you've got is a solution to the problem you have with staffing right now, but also a longer-term solution." Geraci resorts to a sports metaphor to drive his point home. "I think you have to hire good athletes, but they have to meet more than the needs of the job that you have. You're not hiring someone because she is a great 3rd baseman; you are hiring her because she is a great athlete and she can play any position over time. She is more valuable to you because she can play in many positions. This is what I am looking for and what defines the MVP in the recruiting process."

Creating the Job and Person Description

The key to success for bringing in the MVP is to be absolutely clear on what the position is and what type of person you require to fill it. This means knowing:

- the critical success factors for the job
- the critical competencies that are needed, that is, the skills, knowledge and experiences that the candidate should ideally have
- what kind of candidate would fit in with the peer group and its dynamics
- the deliverables and required results
- what kind of candidate would fit in with the culture of the organization
- why people have failed or succeeded in the past

Only when clarity on these issues has been achieved will it be possible to formulate effective interview questions and discover whether a candidate is right for the job.

If used, it is helpful to create a person and job description to guide HR departments and recruitment firms in their search. The job and person description is a detailed document that outlines the following information about the position

- a brief summary of the job
- the key relationships that the person will have
- the major responsibilities, expected results and critical success factors

- the key competencies required and the previous experience the person should have
- the ideal profile of the person who will fill the job

Appendix C gives an example of a detailed job and person description.

Job descriptions are created in a variety of ways.

✓ Find out from existing job holders what they do, the results they achieve and the knowledge and skills required to fill the job.

✓ If the job is a new one, a team of people needs to give input into the job description in terms of the duties and responsibilities, goals and results, and skills and knowledge required. The input would come from the strategic and business plans in terms of the future business growth and projections and from the key people who would work with the new MVP. These key people will give input as to what they expect of the person doing the job in terms of results, and what skills and experiences they expect the person to have.

✓ Spend time focusing on the ideal person and how he or she would fit into the organization. Think about the management style the person will have, and the type of people he or she will be working with as peers and direct reports.

Sources of Candidates

Once the job and person description has been crafted, it is necessary to track down MVP candidates. While this task can be left to a search firm, it can also be pursued internally by drawing on networks of contacts. As we noted in Chapter 3, MVPs are usually very well known in their industry or profession. According to Virginia Murray, Managing Director of A.T. Kearney Executive Search, "It's pretty easy to identify them because people say this is a really great guy and their reputation usually precedes them, so they are not hard to identify." Dan Geraci of Phoenix Investment Partners concurs. "If you are good at being involved in your industry and you've got a good network of people in the industry, you will know who the talented people are." Seth Wolk, head of HR for J. Walter Thompson, points out that often he doesn't just know of an MVP but has already established a relationship. "You get these long-term pursuits. Meet with them now, and get someone else to meet with them six months from now. Suggest to them that when they are in London, in another six months, they meet with this person from JWT. That way you develop long-term relationships."

Robin Burns, Chief Executive Officer of Intimate Beauty Corporation, Victoria's Secret Beauty and aura Science gives an example of sourcing candidates from people she had worked with successfully in the past, and who proved to be successful in their new roles. "I was President of Calvin Klein Cosmetics in 1983, and it was my first time as a CEO. I had an opening for someone to run the manufacturing plant and I had never run a manufacturing business before. I found a candidate with the right experience and hired him. I said to him, 'Look, Sam, don't ever let us be out of stock on the important products that we're trying to ship. Don't ever surprise me. Make me a partner.' It was kind of a simple handshake that way. He worked with me in building Calvin Klein from US$6 million to almost US$600 million. Then I went to Estée Lauder as President and he stayed on at Calvin Klein and kept doing great. When I moved here I was delighted to know that he had joined the company a few years before I did and so we now work together again. He has just continued to grow and astound me with his ability to self-teach his standards on quality, on committed time, and on his ability to negotiate with proprietors, to forge great relationships, to surround himself with talent, and be so dedicated and committed to the brand and to our vision of the future."

Search firms can be useful. For Dan Geraci, they are "good at finding or surfacing people with a particular skill." But he cautions that "a resume does not show you what's between that person's ears or in their heart." In general, Geraci says, "If you need a search firm to find you the best people in your industry, then you've been spending too much time in your office! I've always been a firm believer that you should know who the best people are."

The Interview Process

The interview is a critical part of selection, allowing the organization to assess the potential of the candidate, and the candidate to assess the suitability of the organization. It is essential that interviewers are very clear about the skills and abilities required for the current job and for potential opportunities. They also need to be clear about the type of person that will fit in at the organization.

The need to look for a cultural fit was stressed by many people we interviewed, since an inability to adapt to the organization's culture is a key reason for MVP failure. The comments of Sue Lueger, head of HR for Northwestern Mutual, are typical. "The question we ask ourselves up front is, is this person going to be a fit for us and are we going to be a fit for this person? We are looking for someone who can come here and do a good job, and have the same kind of values that we have.... If this person is all for themselves, and they just want to move up as quickly as possible and don't care who they step on, it doesn't matter how valuable they are—we don't want them here. We put a lot of work into identifying what kind of person we want, and we do tend to look at hiring this person as if they are going to stay here for the rest of their career."

Other managers we talked to addressed the question of how to structure the process effectively. Mary Ann Tocio, President and COO of Bright Horizons Family Solutions, explains that she uses an individual interview and then a group interview and discussion to determine if the person will fit into the company. "I interview people one on one. Then another way to find out if people will fit in this culture is to get them in a group interview to be part of a discussion. I really want to get that person into a discussion. We explain one of our challenges to them and then see how the person contributes to the discussion. This is how we work when people are in the organization, so if they are going to be a misfit it will be glaringly obvious pretty quickly." Lou de Ocejo, Executive Vice President of Human Resources and Organizational Performance at State Street, talks about the need for the candidate to meet with multiple people during the interview process. "I rely on a multitude of people in the organization being exposed to the individual. I think that's both good for the individual so that they can make a better and more informed decision and likewise for the organization."

Another key to successful selection is to set up interviews with influential people in the organization. Once the person is recruited, these influential people then have a stake in making that person successful and helping him or her with the assimilation process. Diane Hessan, President and CEO of Communispace, notes that she is part of the final stages of the interview process with key people she wants to hire. Being interviewed by the CEO shows candidates that she is serious about hiring the person, and giving them all the information she can to allow them to make an informed decision. "If I find someone who has a lot of promise and they've been working for 20 years, I'll interview them. I spend over an hour with those who are in the final stages of recruiting and I'll tell them everything I can about the company. I tell them that they have passed all my tests and have the capability to do the job. I then say, 'If you think you can be successful in this company and in this job, I want to lay out everything I can and I want you to tell me whether you think this is the game that you can win.' I do overload them on the situation of the company and the culture. We are an entrepreneurial organization, and I know a ton of talented people who wouldn't make it here."

The Reference Check

A vitally important part of the selection process is the reference check. Many organizations do not do full reference checks and find out later that they made a mistake. It is necessary to speak to the candidate's references and also to contacts in the industry or profession who may have some insights into how the candidate may fit into your organization. This should be relatively straightforward, since MVPs are well known in their industry or profession. References and contacts should be asked the very questions put to candidates during interviews. The reference check will then contribute to determining key competencies of candidates, their possible blind spots and their likely fit with the organization. The intent of the reference check is to ensure that the MVP will be successful.

Some managers rely heavily on reference checks, in combination with factual measures, to determine a candidate's suitability. Lou de Ocejo of State Street, for example, speaks of his reliance on precisely this combination of "empirical tools" and references. "Show me the numbers and show me the norms. How does this person's profile match against a particular group? Assessment is a key for me in terms of a benchmark. I'm talking about checking for those things like intellectual horsepower, curiosity, social skills and interpersonal abilities. I need insurance and I need it on a factual basis. I'm a big believer that references, if done well and appropriately, can also serve as part of the recipe in making a good decision. I would say good, thorough screening and interviewing, followed up by assessment, followed up by references, are key, all preceded by a good definition of the job and good definition of the individual."

Do What It Takes to Get Them

Even after a company has done everything right and truly found the perfect candidate for the job, failure remains a distinct possibility—not, in this instance, a failure of the candidate to meet expectations but of the company to hire the candidate in the first place. In short, no matter how perfect for the job, an MVP may simply say no to an offer. It is vitally important, therefore, to do whatever it takes to get the MVP to take the position.

This may mean that policies and approaches have to be bent or broken, and that the individual's personal situation needs to be taken into account. As Ian Hendry, head of HR for

RBC Capital Markets comments, "If we are trying to upgrade our talent pool and identify someone who can potentially generate multimillion dollars of business, are we going to cut some slack? Of course we are. Within reason, we will try and do everything we can to accommodate them. However, not every hire is a franchise player. Are we going to do the same thing for a journeyman? Of course we're not. We've talked about an evolution to mass customization for some time now and more simply put, this is about practical HR management."

Doing what it takes may also mean being decisive. Gordon Bethune, Chairman and CEO of Continental Airlines, hired Larry Kellner as his President and COO a mere 10 minutes into their interview. "I was just blown away by him," recounts Kellner. "Within 10 minutes, he went from who are you to how do I get you to take the job. Then within an hour he said, 'Your wife needs to come down here and have dinner with me a week from Friday night, because we need to know if she will like Houston.' He immediately cut right to the chase. What blew me away was that I would have told you the odds that I'd come to work here were 5%. But on the flight going home I was 95% sure I'd work here. Here was a guy who asked me a couple key questions, jumped on a few things I said, and then said that I was what he was looking for and he knew I'd fit there." Clearly Bethune recognized the importance of being decisive and of getting not only Kellner but his wife to buy into the decision. Of course, he had done his due diligence prior even to contacting Kellner.

Optimizing the Assimilation Process

As we discussed at length earlier, the newly recruited MVP's ability to meet the organization's expectations depends as much on a successful process of assimilation as on a successful process of selection. Mark Snyder of State Street notes that it can take as long as six months to integrate a new person into the culture of the company. State Street recognizes the need to manage the process, at least informally. "Our job," says Snyder, "is to point them in the right direction, answer a lot of questions and give them guidance. We also help them understand the culture here. We expose them to internal people and customers and to different people in different parts of our business, and given that we are organized along global business unit lines, typically in different locations around the world."

At many organizations, helping MVPs assimilate is low on the list of priorities. As Bill O'Grady, head of Distribution and Sales at Pioneer Investments, comments, "Most times people say, 'This is a player, this is a hitter, this is an MVP and you can just bring them in and turn them loose and it's going to work.'" O'Grady feels that "more time needs to be spent with MVPs to make sure that the expectation levels align." We agree.

A number of assimilation or integration activities must be engaged in if MVPs are to start off on the right foot with the team, manage resistance to change and build credibility in the organization. This section will consider three key on-boarding stages essential to ensuring the newly recruited MVP's ultimate success:

- identifying the few key objectives
- creating an appointment charter
- building stakeholder relationships and ongoing stakeholder management

    Bringing our discussion to a close, we will also consider:

- the resources that may be available to assist MVPs with their integration

Identifying the Few Key Objectives

In order to be viewed as creating value for the organization, the newly hired MVP should first and foremost identify and get agreement on the few key objectives that must be accomplished within the first six months. Agreement on the two or three critical objectives and required performance standards should be reached in conjunction with the manager and the critical stakeholders. This is not as easy as it sounds because various stakeholders may present the MVP with conflicting expectations, different or hidden agendas and differing assumptions. In such circumstances, the MVP must strive to achieve and confirm agreement on critical objectives among all key stakeholders. Lack of such an agreement can easily derail the new MVP.

Creating an Appointment Charter

Once the MVP has identified the key few objectives, he or she writes them into an appointment charter. This charter is a formal document that encourages the manager, the MVP and key stakeholders to be explicit about the requirements of the job, its challenges and the few key objectives that will be critical in measuring performance and success in the first six months or so.

The appointment charter must focus on three key areas:

- **The Role**. This covers the scope of the responsibilities, the few critical objectives that must be achieved, together with the time frames and deadlines, and the key authorities associated with the role.

- **The Relationship**. This identifies the support that the MVP requires from his or her manager, the key relationships that have to be managed, and ways to get feedback from the manager and key stakeholders.

- **The Development**. This identifies the key people who need to be recruited as coaches and mentors in order to help the MVP navigate his or her way in the new culture, together with any opportunities for speeding up learning, such as attending key conferences or meetings.

The creation of the charter allows the MVP to meet with all key stakeholders and to get agreement as to what is expected of him or her. Whether or not a formal document is produced, it is essential that the MVP finds out the information noted above, and updates it continually.

APPOINTMENT CHARTER TEMPLATE

Date:
New Leader's Name:
Reports to:

I. Role Focus

I A Scope of Responsibilities—summarize key responsibilities

I B Few Key Objectives—identify the three to four accomplishments and results that must be achieved by the new MVP, together with time frames and any deadlines

I C Decision-Making Authority—outline specific authority for budgets, hiring, contracts and other signing authority

II. Relationship Focus

II A Support Required from the MVP's Manager—detail ways that the manager can support the achievement of objectives

II B Other Key Relationships to Manage—give names of key stakeholders in the organization and external to the organization

II C Preliminary Feedback Plan—detail regular communication channels and frequency of communication with manager and stakeholders

III. Development Focus

III A Key People Resources—outline the names and positions of key people who might act as coaches, mentors and supporters

III B Potential Opportunities for Speeding up Learning—detail meetings, training programs, conferences that may help with learning

Building Stakeholder Relationships and Ongoing Stakeholder Management

Building and maintaining relationships with key stakeholders is an important part of the MVP's work. Stakeholders can be located inside the organization or can be outsiders, such as customers and vendors. MVPs should look to their managers and HR departments to help them identify essential relationships that need to be created and sustained. Building such relationships is crucial if MVPs are to avoid significant resistance to what they are trying to achieve. Kevin Wassong of J. Walter Thompson notes, "One of the things that we do for people who come in and are viewed as MVPs is to set up a lot of time for them to meet with all the other people who we think are critical to the operation. We line them up with the right people within the organization to get a gauge of what has worked and what has not worked. And we give them the framework and access to people who can help guide their growth down the line."

Mentors can often help the MVP overcome resistance, especially from internal people who did not get the job. They can help bring the MVP up to speed on the cultural and political realities of the organization and can alert the new person to behaviors and approaches that are not acceptable in this organization. David Lissy, CEO of Bright Horizons Family Solutions, describes his mentoring activities. "When I bring people into the company, I talk to them about integrating themselves in the company in the right way. I give them coaching about how they can earn their influence. People who are going to try to get their influence by the fact that they report to the CEO will only be here a short time, because that's not the way our culture works." It's essential for an MVP to seek out, and for an organization to provide, the kind of mentoring described by Lissy.

Once relationships with key stakeholders, including mentors, have been forged, MVPs must manage those relationships on an ongoing basis. As we discussed earlier, time frames and expectations can sometimes change without notice. Sustaining an active engagement with stakeholders is the surest means of tracking changing circumstances. Surprises are not normally conducive to MVP success.

Potential Resources Available to the MVP

There are a number of potential resources in any organization that are available to help the new MVP. Identifying and accessing these early on can help MVPs succeed at both meeting expectations and adapting to the new culture. Such resources are:

- the manager
- peers
- members of the team, if the MVP manages a team

- people who were part of the interview process
- people with the same professional background
- those who may have come to this organization from the same company as the MVP
- the HR department
- people who have been identified as formal mentors in the organization
- customers/clients
- external coaches the organization may engage to help with the assimilation of new MVPs

It may take time to track down the appropriate people who can provide informal help, but it is well worth the effort. To build credibility or influence in the organization, MVPs must ensure that they do not become too isolated or invisible.

Summary

This chapter looked at bringing in the MVP from outside the company and covered:

- the reasons why externally recruited MVPs may fail
- optimizing the selection process
- optimizing the assimilation process

Suggested Resources

1. Manchester-MPS Group, *Web Based Toolkit for New Leaders and Supervisors*. 1 Independent Drive, Jacksonville, FL 32202.
2. Dan Ciampa and Michael Watkins, *Right From the Start. Taking Charge in a New Leadership Role* (Boston: Harvard Business Press, 1999).

CHAPTER 7

Managing Difficult MVPs

There is sometimes a tension at the top performance levels. The top performers do what others do not seem capable of doing. They can be seen as action oriented or as aggressive. They can challenge the status quo and they can be disruptive. MVPs can perform at these high levels and yet behave in such a way that builds the organization. And then, sometimes, they slip, creating more problems than they are worth. We have worked with many managers of very valuable performers who have, for various reasons, become disruptive, annoying or unpleasant. We need to remember that MVPs, just like the rest of us, have weaknesses and problems that can show up at work. Hence, managing an MVP who has become difficult is a challenge that managers may encounter.

Dan Geraci, President and CEO of Phoenix Investment Partners, recognizes that managing difficult MVPs is what separates the strongest managers from the rest. "Not all MVPs are angels by any stretch of the imagination. In order to be successful, there is a bit of aggressiveness that is in there and it's not always going to be positive and you have to manage it. There is a reason why MVP is a good term—it's a reference to athletes. Managing a business is like managing a sports franchise. You have all kinds of players who have behaviors that are different; some of them are wild, some of them are choir boys and you have to manage each of them in a way that relates to their skill set and their profile, and yet a common set of standards and behaviors that is acceptable to you has to be enforced. It's what makes managing so much fun. It's the diversity of personalities that you have to be confronted with. No two days are the same."

So, how do you manage a difficult MVP? As you would any other difficult employee, only better. MVPs are important corporate assets and need to be cared for and managed as such. We asked our interviewees if MVPs get special handling. Most said yes, while others only whispered yes. The MVP's value to the organization ups the ante for managers when performance or behavioral problems develop. To understand the problems and cures associated with difficult MVPs, we will look at these four areas:

- Can a difficult person be an MVP?
- Identifying the difficulties
- What a manager can do with a truly difficult MVP
- Taking action

Can a Difficult Person Be an MVP?

In Chapter 3, we argued that MVPs could be identified by such common traits as their tendency to "enhance the company's reputation" and "earn the respect of colleagues." It is fair to say that if such traits do indeed characterize MVPs, then MVPs cannot be difficult people. Difficult people don't normally enhance the company's reputation or gain the respect of colleagues. Our view at the beginning of our research was that just as an apple cannot also be an orange, a difficult employee cannot also be an MVP. At least initially, our interviews corroborated this view. Yet as we delved deeper into the concept of difficult MVPs, we detected a shift in thinking.

Several interviewees made the point that the true MVP has to be a team player and not just an individual achiever of superficially impressive results. Recalling his years as an international consultant, Michael Cohen, President of GeneXP

Biosciences, tells us of one of his client firm's "top producing partners." You could argue he was an MVP because of his economic contribution, but he was not somebody who was a team player or particularly interested in building the firm. He cranked out revenue, year in, year out, and was valuable to the organization because of this. However, his contribution, though significant, was quite narrow and often brought collateral damage with it. If an MVP ultimately is someone who has the ability to have a broad, positive effect on an organization, this partner did not meet the test for MVP." A senior executive we know in the financial services industry speaks in similar terms. "I've seen strong producers who just made other people miserable, but I don't consider that group as part of my MVPs. You can get great results, but if you don't get along with people you are not in that MVP category. For me I need more of a complete package. You could be operating in a top 30 percent category, but you are not going to make it to that top 5 or 10 percent, particularly if what you do angers other people." In general, the views of Cohen and this senior executive are typical of most views we heard on this issue.

However, when we pressed interviewees further, we found a slightly different picture of the MVP emerging. While a difficult employee is unlikely to acquire the stature of an MVP, an existing MVP can sometimes slide into troublesome behavior. "A difficult MVP," says a senior executive, "could come in two colors, if you will. One is that the MVP has become difficult for personal reasons that occur outside of work—family problems, illness, changing personal desires and other such issues. The other is that it's your issue, as a leader, of being able to deal with that particular MVP." Such an MVP, that is, may become difficult because of the way he or she is managed. There are, in fact, any number of reasons why an MVP may become difficult—a long record of success may begin to go to an MVP's head or an MVP may begin to care more about his or her status than about the welfare of the company. The key point is that over time an MVP may lose his or her former effectiveness.

A new question arises: Do you expend the effort to retrieve a once-invaluable person? An executive that we know thinks that you should. "By definition, if it's an MVP creating problems, then it's somebody that's worth saving. The advice that I give is that it's worth the effort, and it's not only worth the effort, it's fair. It could be that the MVP is misdirected; it could be that his/her goals have changed; or it could be that he or she is very unknowledgeable about how to work with people, how to seek help, how to collaborate. In all those cases, there should be some time spent working with them on how these problems can be resolved. Then, at the end, it should become clear to the MVP, as well as the leader, as to whether it's a salvageable situation." This executive raises fairness as an issue worth considering. It is an interesting concept that many people in business dismiss as soft-headed thinking, yet how managers treat their most valuable people has a great impact on the attitudes of other employees toward the organization. Fairness would mandate that people deserve a "fair shake" if they've been MVPs; they've made great contributions, but they are falling from this elevated status. To be in this situation means a manager may need to extend limits and expend extra effort.

In the balance of this chapter, we will consider the need to distinguish between real and apparent difficult behaviors, ways of determining whether a difficult MVP is redeemable, and actions a manager can take to restore a falling MVP to true MVP status.

Identifying the Difficulties

We have already learned that MVPs can be contrarians whose creativity others can find challenging. To identify when MVPs are truly being difficult to manage, we must first take the time to understand behaviors that are merely disruptive. MVPs are sometimes disruptive for understandable, even good, reasons. Such cases of disruption should not be confused with being difficult.

Confusing Dissatisfaction with Difficulty: Are They in the Wrong Job?

Because of their value, MVPs are mobile. They can take their marbles and head home; or worse, they can join the competition. They have choices to make, and they make one of those choices every day when they decide to come into work. Both authors have worked in many types of businesses and with many MVPs. Creative and wealthy MVPs are the most unstable MVPs to manage. Their creativity tends toward emotional decisions that can be motivated by any number of stimuli—a sunny day or a call from a friend on a beach in Thailand—while concurrently their financial freedom diminishes the need to work to maintain financial security. One of us recalls working with a senior HR executive who supported a group of 50 or more of these creative and wealthy MVPs. She dreaded the Mondays after a holiday or after one of her MVP's vacations. She dreaded "the call" from the MVP saying, "I won't be in today or ever, I'm done." She would have to rally her big guns and figure out how to change the MVP's mind.

When MVPs decide to leave and take their "assets" with them, they aren't so much being difficult as responding to dissatisfaction with their jobs. As Ned Riley of SSgA comments, "When a job feels like a job and the talented people feel like they are working just for the paycheck, it doesn't make for a very successful corporation." Irwin Heller of Mintz Levin has spent his entire career working with highly successful lawyers and the past six years managing the firm. He has worked with more than his share of unhappy lawyers and he shares his view of what makes an MVP unhappy and makes him or her consider leaving. "I see the unhappiness caused by one of the following:

1. **They get no respect**. They're not seen for the superstar that they believe they are; they're not asked about decisions relating to the firm or their practice. So, it's a feeling of not getting the respect that their stardom requires, or should require.

2. **Failure to agree to the vision of the firm**. The firm decides it's very comfortable being a one-city firm. But the lawyer's practice is national in scope or he wants to be national or international in scope, so the firm's vision doesn't fit his particular needs. That will drive him out.

3. **The culture in other ways is not the same as what they're looking for**. Here's an example. We had a very significant producer who left, as it turns out with our blessings, because her view was that employees are employees and how you treat them is really not an issue. They are expendable and if they don't like it, we'll find somebody else. I want what I want, when I want it. Our view is much different. We've talked for years about the Mintz Levin family.

"So each lawyer decides what kind of firm he or she wants. It is not just about the money; it's about clients and client service and has something to do with their view of the atmospherics. Those are the top three reasons people leave." MVPs become disruptive and sometimes even leave when they cease to fit in or no longer feel they belong. Compensation is normally not the overriding issue.

MVPs may even have a lower tolerance for dissatisfaction than the general employee population. As Marc Capra, Chief Operating Officer, New York, at J. Walter Thompson, relates, "My own motto is if I come to work four days in a row and I'm not happy, I change my job. That's it. All I will take is four days." We asked him if he ever had four unhappy days in a row and he told us that he never lets it get past two days before doing what is necessary to improve the situation. MVPs identify and challenge problems earlier than most.

When MVPs decide to leave, their manager and their HR person must scramble to learn what the problem is at work and what has proven attractive elsewhere. They then decide what can be done. As Chairman of his company, John Humphrey saw one of his responsibilities as throwing himself in front of the door to prevent an MVP from leaving. "One of the things I did that I think is controversial is I worked my ass off at keeping people. I mean *I worked my ass off at keeping people.* When they would come in and say to me that they were leaving, I just took that as a signal that they were experiencing some dissatisfaction. I met with them. I met with their husbands or wives. I wrote them letters."

Managers need to look past the immediate dissatisfaction and see the root causes of a problem. Helen Sayles of Liberty Mutual gives two examples. "There are some times when you have to say, "This is just not the place for you," or sometimes they are ready to move before we are ready to move them. I won't say that their needing or wanting to move causes a problem; it creates an opportunity because in some cases it forces us to look at people who are blockers and move them out of the way. So, it's an issue and it's a challenge. I wouldn't call it a problem." The challenge, we should note, is not a matter of dealing with a difficult MVP but of finding a proper role for the MVP. MVPs have to be placed in positions where they can thrive.

The MVP as Early Warning System

In the 1950s, *Lassie* was a popular television show. It told the stories of a nice farm family and their dog. In every episode some tragedy threatened the family—Timmy, the boy, fell into a well, or perhaps the barn was on fire. Each tragedy was averted by Lassie loudly barking and drawing the attention of the parents to the danger. They understood that when Lassie barked she was warning them and they should listen. If Lassie had been considered just another noisy animal and her family locked her up, the show would not have lasted more than two or three episodes. MVPs are sometimes a bit like Lassie—"difficult" simply because they are looking out for the larger interests of the organization. They bark at problems that constrain organizational performance.

Smart managers listen to the problems identified by MVPs and rely on them to troubleshoot. Keith Brown of FiRE + iCE depends on the commotion that MVPs create. "They question the guidance I give them, they give me great feedback on the operation, they tell me when I'm off base and they confirm when I make the right decisions. So, that's a big part of why they're important. I mean, I don't really need a yes-man." Lou de Ocejo of State Street expects MVPs to shake the place up. "They usually are the ones that create a lot of problems and they create problems because they tend to pursue things doggedly, especially ideas. They can be not only persistent, but insistent. They tend to be incredibly opinionated. Because they generally have broad interests they get into other people's space. The fact is that if you want some of these folks around, you've got to put up with a little bit of dysfunctionality; it's variety that people perceive in some cases as being dysfunctional." What may seem dysfunctional or difficult may only reflect originality. The difficult MVP may be the manager's best friend.

Unfortunately, not all managers value MVPs' independent thinking. Gerry Lupacchino of Novations/J. Howard & Associates relates an unhappy yet enlightening story from a prior employer. "An MVP may cause problems in an organization when leadership is unwilling to innovate, or when it's fearful of change, that is, by people other than themselves. A gentleman that I used to work for said to me, 'You're like a dog barking at my back door. You've always got something that you see we can do better or differently, and I just wish you'd go out in the yard and sleep.' And I was thankful to him for making it really clear about what my value was to his organization. And I got it at that moment. I got it. I got that if that man stayed at the helm, the organization was going to be exactly the way it looked like today in three years from now and five years from now, because there was such a dramatic and intense resistance to innovation and change. And what I got was I didn't want to work for a company that didn't innovate or change, because we would go stale. How do you create a competitive advantage unless you are willing to continuously improve? And the concept of continuous improvement was so painful to him that he made it crystal clear that I could not add value in our relationship. And at that moment, I started considering other options."

Managers should listen to their MVPs but that does not mean that they should just abdicate their leadership responsibilities and do whatever the MVP is recommending. Use an MVP's identification of a problem as a starting point for critical thought. Tom Kochan, Professor at the MIT Sloan School of Management, was asked if MVPs ever created problems. "Oh sure, by identifying problems that are already under the surface and making them visible and then moving them forward. Let me give you a good example. MIT got a lot of publicity because of a study of women in science a couple of years ago. It was done by the women in the School of Science and raised the issue that the women weren't getting the kind of respect and support in our school that they deserve, and in fact their numbers hadn't increased. They brought this problem to the Provost who said, 'Show me the data.' They showed the Provost the data and they were right—there was a problem. MIT not only stood up to the issue, but they said they were going to do this same study in all the other schools—management, humanities, engineering, urban studies and architecture—and see if they would find similar kinds of things. Now this report, just as it was about to be released to the faculty, got to *The New York Times* and it created this big storm of publicity, but it became very positive publicity because the storyline was that MIT was facing this problem, and it created momentum. Now nothing would have happened if the women in the School of Science weren't willing to show the problem to the Provost and put a little pressure on him to recognize the problem and act. This is exactly what MVPs are expected to do, which is to identify problems and help solve them."

Know Your MVPs and Their Unique Problems

By definition, MVPs are in many ways different than people who make up the general employee population. These differences elevate their value and distinguish them from the crowd. It is reasonable to expect that they may also create friction with others. For example, one of the problems that managers find when MVPs surface issues is how others view the MVP's motives. "I think MVPs can be seen as difficult because they challenge barriers; they challenge practices; they don't necessarily accept resistance; they can be perceived as politically motivated by others; they can be perceived as just trying to look out for themselves," says John Marrs of SSgA. Managers may find themselves defending MVPs to those who are being challenged. We did find that one of the distinguishing features of MVPs is that they have the ability to get others to like them and even follow them, yet some MVPs still may engender problems that can be expected and mitigated early on.

Understanding the nature of the individual MVP and working to support that MVP is a managerial imperative. For Helen Sayles of Liberty Mutual, that support may require little more than providing timely counsel. "In some cases you've got MVPs who are really rule breakers and sometimes they can be very dysfunctional. If they are truly MVPs, they will understand that and they will back off at the right time. They will know when to push and when to...I won't say back off, because MVP's should never back off, but when they'll choose to retreat. It's a good lesson for them. There are times when you have to say, 'You are right, but this is not the time.' We look on that as a challenge and as a learning opportunity to see if they've got the diplomatic skills to be able to judge that."

Knowing the organization in which they function does reduce the potential for MVP-related problems. Audra Bohannon of Novations/J. Howard & Associates sees the key as knowledge of the business goals as well as its culture. "You have to be in alignment to some degree. There is plenty of room for you to have your own personality, but philosophically you want to be in alignment with your organization."

Managers need to help create that alignment. "When I bring people into the company," says David Lissy, CEO of Bright Horizons Family Solutions, "I talk to them about integrating themselves in the company in the right way. I give them coaching about how they can earn their influence." Managers can teach MVPs how to avoid cultural minefields while still moving the company forward. It is a great way to manage difficulties even before they turn into problems.

In general, viewing MVPs as a group of like-minded people that respond to the same management style is a quick way for a manager to run into trouble. A comment made to us by a respected senior HR executive is that "One of the things about MVPs is that not all MVPs are created equal." David Lissy takes the time to learn about each MVP and to consider what each one needs from management. "I'm the kind of manager who, once we work together, will let you have a lot of room to do your thing. The truth is, you earn that right." John Humphrey, formerly of Forum, tells us of some of the company's talented resource network trainers who would do great work out in the field for three days a week and then "come back to the office and make trouble for two days. Had they gone fishing or something for two days, they wouldn't make trouble at the office, and they'd do a better job teaching the next day." The answer? Keep them out of the office.

MVPs face special problems. If they respond to those problems disruptively, they should be appropriately managed, not dismissed as being difficult.

What a Manager Can Do with a Truly Difficult MVP

To this point in the chapter we have looked at how well-meaning MVPs can create disruptions by the very nature of their ability to see problems and respond to challenges. A manager's first and best approach with these MVPs is to make them aware of the problems and offer them MVP-like means to fix them. MVPs will take the challenge and fix the problem. It is now time to take a step into the netherworld of MVPs, where we must consider whether a difficult person can return to being an MVP or whether this person must be dismissed as a net liability. We will look at three broad questions:

- Has the MVP developed poor interpersonal skills or turned malevolent?
- How motivated is the MVP by status and self-interest?

- In general, is the MVP's value overshadowed by his or her liabilities?

Has the MVP Developed Poor Interpersonal Skills or Turned Malevolent?

In years past, one of us was frequently asked by client companies to work out disputes regarding alleged sexual harassment. These situations were terrible for everyone. They almost always involved a male manager and a female subordinate tied together by job roles and great discomfort. The first question we asked of the senior manager and HR manager was "What happened?" This was quickly followed by "Do you think it was intentional?" and "Why or why not?" For us, the question of intention is critical. It determines when dismissal is called for and when an attempt to redeem someone is appropriate. In cases where social ineptness was the issue (and almost always in our experience that was the issue), the resolution usually entailed clearing the communications, coaching the man on social skills and implementing a distancing of the work environment. For clarity we want to reinforce that lack of intention should not be used to excuse the pain and discomfort felt by the person experiencing the harassment, but is relevant when considering remedial action.

The difference between a malevolent person and a socially inept person is intention. A nasty person knows about, and even plans on, creating discomfort for others with the intention of getting them to do things that they would not do under normal circumstances. Examples in a business setting could include:

- having one person compromise another person's chances for promotion
- finding ways to "steal" opportunities from others
- corrupting policies and procedures, as in Enron executives telling people to cook the books and not tell anyone
- creating rumors of others' misdeeds and breaking down trust among peers to further their own plans

So, intention is the deciding factor used to determine whether a troublesome MVP is simply inept or actually malevolent.

However, determining intention is fraught with difficulty. While managers are usually told to avoid this judgment call, it is our experience that, advisable or not, managers *do* make this determination. In the real world we know that we must deal with what actually occurs and not with what should be. Given this context, to "determine intention" asks the manager to form an opinion after careful consideration of what is known. It does not mean that the manager should determine guilt and punishment. It also does not mean that the manager's determination is correct. Managers dealing with a difficult behavioral problem should not go it alone but rather should seek out advice. Good advice will help the manager decide how to proceed. The best advice will come from a manager's best colleagues in upper management, HR and possibly the legal department. HR may also bring in an outside consultant who is experienced in the situation. This can become the manager's internal consulting team. Remember, the manager is forming an opinion because it is unlikely that he or she can uncover the relevant facts. Once the manager has enlisted the internal team, its members can work together to come to a reasoned conclusion about whether an MVP has become manipulative or malevolent, or has simply displayed poor interpersonal skills.

Once a conclusion has been reached, the manager must act. If MVPs are intentionally creating problems to further their own agenda, then call them on it and transfer or fire them. If they are socially inept, then make them aware of it and the problems that it creates for them and for the organization. Sue Lueger, Vice President of Human Resources at Northwestern Mutual, provides valuable guidance on just what a manager might say. "You might be very smart and you might be very technically competent, but if you can't relate to people, or if you're overly aggressive, or whatever it is, it doesn't matter—you're still not going to move ahead. I think sometimes we have to be direct with competent people and say, 'You know, you are really talented and you really have a lot to offer, but these are the issues.'"

How do you decide that an MVP is a bad apple, a bad influence or just plain nasty? You ultimately have to ask yourself whether the value that a difficult MVP produces is depleted by the havoc created. As Dan Geraci, CEO of Phoenix Investment Partners, says describing his understanding of MVPs gone bad, "It will typically show up in them being abusive, stepping outside the bounds, trying to get away with things, using their position as a stick. You will typically find it's when they start mistreating other people or they have taken liberties that have put the firm at risk—the reputation of the business—and that's happened more than once. This is where your own values get called into question as a manager, executive or CEO, where you have to say that no one is bigger than the organization. I don't want anyone sitting around and saying, 'If I did that, I'd be out of here. This guy does it because he's a big hot dog and they keep him—they'll look the other way.' That's what builds that 'us versus them' mentality in your associate base, and if anything I move more quickly to get rid of those people than I would someone who's less of an MVP or less visible in the organization or less senior. The message it sends is powerful."

How Motivated Is the MVP by Status and Self-Interest?

Everyone is motivated to work by something. Most people work to generate enough income to maintain or improve their way of life. Others work to support their way of life *and* because they enjoy what they do. We found that highly motivated employees, including MVPs, work for the same reasons *plus* they find their work to be passionately meaningful. A powerful force is created when you marry the top performance of an MVP with their passions *and* these passions are aligned with the vision of the organization.

But if the MVP's passions and the organization's vision are misaligned, you generate an explosive force. Ned Riley of SSgA has seen many great players lose because they could not reconcile their goals with the business's goals. "The self-absorption factor supercedes the corporate goal. Eventually these people are asked to leave." When MVPs become obsessed with status and self-interest, they lose their value as MVPs and can rarely be redeemed. Managers must know when the line has been crossed. Generally, MVPs are beyond rescue when they become obsessed with ego, power and money.

Recognizing the Malevolent MVP: Ego

Big egos have built and have destroyed many big careers. Aside from generally annoying people who come into contact with it, a big ego can destroy high-level work. Big egos discount and eventually diminish honest feedback and thought offered by others. When you are the best, people with big egos think, why do you need lesser talent questioning your ideas? They are just slowing the big ego down. Normal channels of business intelligence dry up as others learn to couch news in terms that sound like agreement with the "big boss." They have seen what has happened to others who dare to question a master. In receiving less challenging ideas, the big ego receives less valuable information.

Let's be clear on what we mean by the term "ego." We are not positing an expansive psychological term. We are simply saying that "big ego" describes *a person with an exaggerated sense of self-importance*. People with an inflated view of themselves should consider this thought: "Any time you think you have influence, try ordering around someone else's dog."[1]

Some of our interviewees have their own terms for describing these status hogs. Sandy West of Limited Brands calls them "divas." Another interviewee who had been the Chairman of the Board of a large company thinks about them this way: "Prima donnas don't make it as MVPs. However, there very certainly are some MVPs that develop an exaggerated sense of self-importance. It can be very difficult when you are an MVP. Many times you are looked at by many thousands of people as being their leader, their guide, and that sometimes affects the

---

[1] This insight comes from *The Cockle Bur*, a monthly publication by Cockle Printing Company. The recent issue can be viewed at www.cocklelaw.com.

ego. That probably is one of the more difficult things to try to manage."

John Carey of Pioneer Investments has seen successful people fall in love with themselves. "We've had some people over the years who have probably shared some of the prima donnas' characteristics and by and large they are gone and they did cause problems. They were very demanding sometimes and they lost sight of the job they were supposed to do, and in some cases even damaged the company. Leaving was usually a mutual agreement and it was usually over a short period of time. In every case I would say there was a long period of development where the people enjoyed success and grew in their skill set and then there was some critical moment when they passed over to prima donna status. Usually the period of development was much longer than that prima donna period because they crashed and burned pretty quickly in every case."

That there was some critical moment "when they passed over to prima donna status" is an important idea. If a manager can catch that moment and point it out to the MVP, then the damage may be halted. It is an unusual manager that can, in fact, catch that moment, therefore it is best to continue to hold the MVP to a higher standard and point out prima donna behavior whenever it is displayed. One of our interviewees shares a painful experience with one of his top people. "It was a freak accident and a person died. I immediately contacted the Senior Vice President responsible for that division. I wanted to talk to him about how he would communicate it in his business the next day, so we had that conversation, which was appropriate, and very quickly he turned the conversation to how this was going to really screw up his sales and to impact his bonus. That's [prima donna] behavior. And I said to this individual, I'm not even going to engage in that conversation with you. A person is dead, and I understand your concern, but you know, I will tell you, that was totally driven by what's this going to mean to you personally." As you can see, he told the prima donna what he thought and why, with the hope that behavior could be altered.

Recognizing the Malevolent MVP: Power and Money

Many driven people love to measure their success. How many times have you heard that the money doesn't matter, it's just a way of keeping score. This is a benign example unless power and money are viewed as part of a zero-sum game. If power and money are limited resources, then someone has to lose power and money for the MVP to gather it. An MVP has the ability to outperform and outpace most people in an organization; in many ways it is not a fair competition. Would it be fair to have Tiger Woods play tournament golf against a 20-handicap player? Woods would probably beat the high handicap golfer by those 20 strokes and quite likely by another 10 for good measure. Neither would enjoy the lopsided game nor be very motivated to try it again. Recall that MVPs thrive when challenged. Dan Geraci considers the challenge of managing power and money with motivated employees. "These people have big egos that can be difficult to manage. They have to be given more and more difficult goals to achieve to prove that they are in a league of their own."

A senior HR executive has seen the problems created by power hoarding and money grabbing. "Problems begin when they [MVPs] start to believe their own press and think that they can do no wrong and get a little cocky and arrogant. They either tick people off or trip over their own egos, and end up hurting themselves and hurting the organization in the process. They can be demanding—'I want to take a three-month sabbatical,' 'I want this office,' 'I want that job, and if I don't get that job then I'm going to leave,' 'If I have to work for Mary, I'm going to leave,' 'I want this promotion.' They can be very, very demanding." They make themselves into a target that begins to glow as soon as they falter. Their façade of importance fades and their manipulation of management and co-workers becomes visible. Co-workers who have contained their anger at the hoarding and grabbing let them fall; sometimes they will even push them along. Management may also be looking for a way to end the intentionally endless demands and see an opportunity to "give in" and let them leave.

Is an MVP's Value Overshadowed by His or Her Liabilities?

MVPs are a scarce asset. Sometimes a new hire sprints out of the blocks and quickly leads the pack. More often, an MVP has partnered with a good organization where opportunities are available and growth is a core value. It is a mutual investment that can pay off as the MVP and the organization grow. Like any investment, it can also be lost. What you do not want is for the investment to become a sinkhole, with time and money thrown at bad situations. At some point a manager must answer this difficult question: Is it prudent to continue giving special consideration to a "fallen MVP" or do you cut your losses?

The dilemmas facing the manager who's dealing with a fallen MVP are real. An HR executive we spoke to describes them this way: "It is constant…you have to always be thinking *Do I want to give this project to this person? Is that going to make them happy or is that going to make them more miserable? What if they leave in the middle of it?* There are a million questions. It's always an evaluative moment—will they/won't they. I think the other downside is they can preempt projects and take work from other people; they might take on stuff that other people may aspire to. Part of it is believing their own press, the idea of 'I'm so wonderful, you should want to give me everything; I want X, Y and Z.' Then the worst part is the unpredictability, to an extent. This person can go anywhere. How can I be sure that I can provide the things that are going to make him or her want to be here? I can't be in his or her head. There is a lot of care and feeding and *is it really worth it?*"

Interestingly, most managers we interviewed would balk at asking this question, because ultimately they do feel attached to a person whose contribution to the organization has been so extraordinarily good. MVPs are generally very likeable and this positive aura may not fade easily among senior management. A respected MVP in trouble will usually have many people rally around him or her.

Still, at a certain point the question of whether the negative behaviors are outweighing the positive (or the formerly positive) behaviors has to be faced up to. Andrew Faas of Shoppers Drug Mart points out a major liability of a fallen MVP. "Obviously there are some star players out there who become 'prima donnas,' and once that happens their agenda is not aligned with the organization's. More to the point, it creates a problem with the integrated [work] model. We look at it in terms of assets and liabilities and again the inability to work well in an integrated environment far surpasses the star talent category. So, do you sometimes have to let some of those stars go? Yes. It's recognizing that they are star talent but it cannot be at the expense of others."

What if you let a fallen MVP go and he or she lands with the competition? It is never an easy decision, but sometimes making a tough decision ends a bad situation while demonstrating leadership to your other top people. Now your competitor has to manage the talent whose ego smothers others, while you make room for your best people to grow. Your competitor gets your problem and your best people get new opportunities.

So, how does a manager decide that an MVP's value is overshadowed by his or her liabilities? The most critical value of any MVP is his or her superior performance. Does it still exist? If not:

- Does the MVP continue to have residual value as a teacher, leader or as a source of organizational pride?

- Does the organization have an emotional commitment to someone who has done so much to build its success? A value-based organization does not want to use somebody up and then show them the door.

If the answer is no to these questions, then the manager may decide to move the fallen MVP out. Frankly, these questions essentially address the level of co-workers' emotional commitment to the MVP. If the MVP has squandered the emotional commitment that he or she has built over years of dedicated work, then the MVP may deserve to be shown the door. [2]

If the MVP's performance is still strong, then the manager should consider the MVP's impact on others. This can be accomplished by using the basic assets of an MVP:

1. **MVPs are motivated by intrinsic passion**. Does the MVP's passion for the organization's interests continue while diminishing self-interest?

2. **MVPs expect to succeed and do not like to fail**. Does the MVP attempt to succeed while including others in the success?

3. **MVPs show moral courage**. Can the MVP's motivations and actions still be trusted?

4. **MVPs are committed to the values and vision of the company**. Is the MVP still aligned with organization?

5. **MVPs enhance the company's reputation**. Is this still accurate?

6. **MVPs earn the respect of colleagues**. Is this still accurate?

Each *no* answer provides a further indication that the MVP is a liability. Answers become data to be discussed by the manager with his or her team of stakeholders, and contribute to the final decision made by the manager in conjunction with this team.

Taking Action

At some point, a good manager will realize that some direct action must be taken. He or she has tried making a casual

---

[2] We often see MVPs whose behaviors can be traced to untreated emotional problems: depression, bipolar disorders, attention deficit disorders, addictions, extended family problems and others. The behaviors have depleted the tolerance of co-workers but could be professionally diagnosed and treated, resulting in the return of a highly valued person and the resurrection of goodwill. To consider this possibility, managers should determine what resources are available within their organization to manage such issues (HR, medical, employee assistance resources or community services).

comment to the MVP about his or her impact on others or has attempted a more formal discussion designed to turn the MVP around. Now an action plan that includes contingency options needs to be devised. The following actions, in this order, are recommended:

- assess the situation
- know your limits
- prepare a plan

Assess the Situation

One of us worked with the new President of a business unit of a large company. The company had a competent but fractious senior management team that had seen two other Presidents come and go. The team, while competent, was constantly stirred up by the high-flying head of sales, "Tom." This guy had proven his ability to deliver but did so at a high cost to others. He was a demeaning poor listener who gathered credit and shunned responsibility. He made it clear that only he held the keys to the marketplace. Tom had also studiously curried favor with key corporate players. The new President allowed the situation to continue for six months while he studied his options. He tested the market by calling on colleagues to determine Tom's true value to the customers. He also carefully kept the key corporate players up to date on the problems and on his attempts to resolve them. After six months he went to the corporate players and explained his thoughts and his course of action; they agreed. The next Monday morning he fired Tom. Tom made the rounds at the corporate level only to find that his key supporters commiserated with him but would not second-guess the decision. Tom made noise but was gone by Wednesday. The President rebuilt the team and maintained the sales course. Within one year, sales had tripled.

As this story clearly shows, it is wise to assess the situation carefully before taking action, whether that action involves dismissing the fallen MVP or attempting to redeem him or her. A fallen MVP may believe that he or she is untouchable because the business rides on his or her shoulders. In most situations this perception is based on past performance and does not take into account current problems that diminish value. Time is usually on the manager's side because it allows the fallen MVP to demonstrate the disruptive behaviors and the manager to think through his or her options carefully. Managers need to accept that it is incumbent on them to make a case for action with the fallen MVP's supporters. The manager has daily contact with the problem person, while other senior executives have infrequent and often manipulated experiences with the person; hence, the often-heard comment "he is good at managing up." With time on his side, the manager can draw on the expertise of others. He or she can assemble a team that could include senior management, HR, a content area expert and as needed, expert consultants in the law, business psychology/coaching, outplacement and/or recruiting. Backed up by such a team, the manager can then swing into action, either setting out conditions for the MVP's improvement or ending the business relationship.

Know Your Limits

How far are you willing to go? Is ending the business relationship truly an option? Putting out a fallen MVP can be a major step that should be the result of a risk/reward analysis. The risk is losing a valued asset, but how valued at this point? Some people just must be kept—they may have an important reputation in the marketplace; they may own a lot of stock; the Board of Directors or the Founder may "owe" this person for all the previous good works; or the person may be the President's relative. For good reasons or bad, sometimes they must stay; the risk, and the expense, of putting them out may be too great. On the other hand, the manager may find that the risk is so low that the fallen MVP's leaving may not even cause a ripple.

What is the potential reward? As we saw in the story we just told, the internal working environment may improve after the difficult MVP leaves. We have seen difficult executives hold whole companies hostage to the threat of leaving—"I own the market" or "Only I know the production process well enough..." Most of the time these are empty boasts used to intimidate senior management. One President told us that it was "like being let out of prison the day after that guy left." If the President feels that way then the co-workers feel it even more.

Many managers do set clear limits. Speaking of an MVP, Diane Hessan of Communispace tells us, "He's created problems from time to time, but not huge ones. If I thought he was being abusive to people, he'd be out of the company. If I thought he was a negative influence on the organization and hurting the culture, he'd be out. If I thought he was doing things that were unethical or disrespectful, he'd be out." Roger Brown, Executive Chairman of Bright Horizons, is clear that quirkiness is manageable while negativity is unacceptable. "I think I have a tolerance for a certain kind of risk and a certain kind of anarchy. For instance, if someone has a really negative attitude and is undermining the culture of the organization, I have zero tolerance for that. That's what anarchy really is. That doesn't work. People constructively disagreeing is terrific, but the stuff I've seen in a lot of organizations I've been in in the past, where unhappy people refuse to fix problems or to go away, is unacceptable. It's an acid that corrodes its container. I think we've tried from the beginning to say, 'Look if it's not working for you, fine, it's a big world.'"

At times the best a company can do is minimize the damage. All problems cannot be solved; some people are just too valuable to the organization even if they create havoc. In these situations the best that can be done is to isolate the person, to put him or her in a box with breathing holes. Work this out carefully.

Prepare a Plan: A 12-Point Checklist for Resolving an MVP Problem

Preparations for action, especially when the aim is to turn around a falling or a fallen MVP, and action itself, should include the following steps:

1. **Identify the specific problems**. Do your research. Determine the specific nature of the problem and assess the harm it does. The manager should try to observe the problem directly rather than relying on secondhand reports.

2. **Document the problem**. Once the problem has been identified, the manager can document it when it occurs. He or she should note problematic behaviors. While opinions can be argued over, factual description of observed behaviors cannot be so easily contested: "You hurt Tony's feelings" is an opinion that can be argued; "You called Tony a jerk" is a factual report. To move from a behavior report to a problem definition, a manager could say, "You called Tony a jerk and we do not accept name-calling in our workplace." Documentation can help the manager show the person the extent of the problem and its impact at work.

3. **Build an action team**. The manager is working with an important asset and should not go it alone. The team can begin with the manager's boss and a trusted HR professional. This team can then decide if other "experts," such as a content area expert and expert consultants in law, business psychology/coaching, outplacement and/or recruiting, should be brought in. The expanded team can then work through the next steps together.

4. **Determine how far senior management is willing to stretch to keep the person, and under what circumstances the company will allow termination**. The team members should understand the parameters that constrain or free their actions.

5. **Identify key supporters and influencers of the falling MVP**. Can they be used to influence the person's behavior or to make the person more accepting of behavior change? Also, keep supporters informed of the plans and the actions if it is likely that the person will seek their influence to derail the plans.

6. **Create a plan of action**. Develop a step-by-step plan of how to corral and manage the falling MVP. What will each member of the team be responsible to manage? Will senior management set strong limits? Here is what Dan Geraci has to say on this topic: "I've had situations where I've had people think that there is just no way I would do it [set strong limits on an MVP]. Maybe it's someone I hired—all the more reason. If anything, that means I'm going to give them an even harder time and really beat 'em about the ears about the fact that you don't put me in a position like this, because I will not stand for it. I will finish it and I will finish it fast and I'll be happy to make an example out of you and, by the way, it's your own doing."

7. **Do a risk/reward analysis**. Using as objective a view as possible, consider what the best and the worst potential outcomes are and then what the likely outcome is. Do these outcomes fall within the organization's acceptable parameters? Modify the plan as needed to get the job done within the set parameters.

8. **Develop "what if" contingencies**. Continually ask the "what do we do if" questions. What do we do if the manager talks with the person and the manager is told that the problem is everyone else? What do we do if the person threatens to call the President to get the annoying manager to stop the harassment? Consider as many of these questions as can be thought of and determine a plan of action for each question. Someone with a sales orientation may be talented at generating the standard objections that a person may use. Don't forget the question "What do we do if the person throws up a question or a roadblock that we have not considered?"

9. **Plan for backfilling the falling MVP's work**. An important contingency that, in our experience, concerns senior management is to know what has been done by the manager to prepare for how the person's current value will be replaced. This may be simple or it may take two or

three employees to take on the job. Have this contingency plan in hand.

10. **Review and finalize the plan with the key players**. Keep people informed and modify the plan as required. This process requires good management skills— if you have them, use them; if you do not have them, get them! It is better to ask for help as you manage a fallen MVP than it is to later ask for forgiveness.

11. **Act**. Know what you are going to do and to say, and also know why you are taking this action. When you talk with the fallen MVP, be prepared to:

    a. State the problem as you and your support team see it.

    b. Provide behavior-based examples of the stated problems.

    c. Listen to the fallen MVP and avoid engaging in defending your position.

    d. Tell the fallen MVP what he or she can do to regain high status. Be as specific as possible, using behavioral examples of positive action.

    e. Develop a mutually agreed-to set of goals and a method for identifying progress and regression. Create a plan for improvement and for follow up.

12. **Follow through**. Do not back off. Use the momentum that you have worked hard to create to come to resolution.

This 12-point plan can help you to structure your approach to saving a fallen MVP.

Don't Avoid the Problem Altogether

It would be great if managers could intervene in the early stages of all employee problems, but frankly this is unlikely. Most managers have too many employees and responsibilities to keep track of employees' performance on a frequent basis. Managers do have the time, or should make the time, to keep an eye on the small percentage of the employees who are

MVPs. Managers would never leave without taking a few minutes to check to make sure that the shop's doors are locked. It doesn't take much more time to check on the status of the 2 percent to 10 percent of the employees who are MVPs. Short bursts of communication spread over time go a long way.

The retired Chairman of a publicly traded company that we know speaks of communicating. "The thing I find most unfortunate in a lot of managers is lack of communication. Communication is so important for a variety of reasons. It's only fair to communicate and it's only fair for the organization, for you as the manager and for the MVP. Being open all the time...not many people take it very well and some MVPs don't want you to be open, but I find it's very important on the manager's side to be very communicative and open and hope that that serves to give a good example on one hand but also to flesh out what's wrong."

Dan Geraci takes the "brutally honest" point to the next level by explaining that MVPs may have to be reprimanded in public. MVPs are visible embodiments of what an organization considers to be its best people. If they violate the culture or embarrass the organization, then others will see the problem and need to see the solution. "This avoids them being seen as the golden-haired child who can get away with anything. *MVPs need to be held to even higher standards than their colleagues.*" A public reprimand needs to be delivered thoughtfully, though, not as an emotional dressing-down at the coffee machine. We asked Geraci how to manage a public reprimand without angering the MVP, and he explains that it has to do with preparation. "It has to be made clear to MVPs when they join an organization that they have to be an example for the rest of the team, and that they will be held to higher standards than others. Thus, you need to tell them up front that you are going to make an example of them if they break the rules, and that you will do this to stop others from feeling that MVPs are untouchable."

An MVP is more than just a good employee; an MVP is a company asset. John Marrs of SSgA describes them as "walking assets that leave the office every evening." An MVP going bad can still be very valuable to an organization. Redeeming the MVP should be a prime objective of any manager. An even more essential objective is to keep the MVP from falling in the first place. We have found that managers become aware of falling behaviors long before they feel the pressure to act. A little thoughtful and direct talk earlier in the process may avoid much of the pain later. Honesty has a way of clearing up confusion. When managing MVPs, managers should remember that important people are watching the management of this corporate asset. It's a high-risk situation but preparing well and getting it right presents great opportunity to shine.

Identify the problems. Don't go it alone—build a team, act, communicate and look around. That is what managing difficult MVPs is about.

Summary

Four topics were covered in relation to managing difficult MVPs:

- can a difficult person be an MVP?

- identifying the difficulties

- what a manager can do with a truly difficult MVP

- taking action

The Role of HR in Managing the MVP

The processes and roles of HR supporting management of the MVP are the subjects of this chapter. While HR plays a number of roles, the primary one highlighted by the HR executives we interviewed involves assisting with the identification and development of MVPs. John Marrs, Senior Vice President of HR for State Street Global Advisors, speaks for many when he tells us, "My role is to facilitate a process to support managers in identifying who the MVPs are, and to make sure that managers have the resources available to help them grow and develop these MVPs. We also have to be the organization's facilitator/ombudsman to make sure that this talent, because it is a corporate talent, doesn't get stuck and has the ability to grow. It may mean an overseas assignment or an assignment in a different discipline in the organization; it may mean a project." Assisting management in the identification and development of MVPs can be analyzed into a number of key HR processes:

- talent assessment
- development processes
- recruitment to fill talent gaps
- recognition and rewards
- HR policies

Talent Assessment

The areas that will be considered in the review of talent assessment are:

- the role of HR
- performance management
- talent review

The Role of HR

HR primarily provides management with performance management and talent review tools to ensure that talent is properly assessed and then developed. Tim Manning, head of HR for NSTAR, calls HR personnel "the shepherds of the talent review process." "Our challenge," he says, "really is to create templates and create opportunities where we can help our management properly assess the resources that are working for them." Helen Sayles, head of HR for Liberty Mutual, comments similarly, "The challenge is to be able to create and facilitate the talent identification process and put in place things that make sure that will happen."

Secondarily, HR must also secure the integrity and objectivity of assessment. Management must be held accountable for outcomes. As Sayles explains, "We enforce accountability because it's too easy sometimes for managers to believe that these processes are just HR things and have little relevance to the business." Manning notes a tendency for talent assessment to descend to the level of anecdotes that merely talk someone up in glowing terms. It is HR's job to see that assessments are "more quantifiable and less anecdotal so that we can understand who those folks are."

In other words, an important part of HR's function is to work with managers at different levels of the organization to make sure that the true talent, the talent of the MVP, is identified. Ruth Wright, a Senior Researcher at the Conference Board of Canada, notes that HR departments are increasingly succeeding at this task. "There are more organizations that are feeling good about what they have been able to achieve in the area of performance management. They have been able to clearly differentiate between the performance of their employees, and in particular feel confident that they are identifying the top performers, and developing and rewarding them in line with their performance grading."

In the aftermath of rigorous assessment, HR's additional function encompasses talent development. Says Tim Manning, "We also have experience in providing advice and counsel around development activities for those folks and how they can help bring them to the next level. We can provide strategies around internal transfers and promotions and other developmental opportunities that really help nurture and retain the talent that we have. We have to create a process where we are not just going to blindly accept someone's evaluation. We need to challenge it and be deliberate and thoughtful about it. If we are going to declare folks to be a certain category and we begin to put in place developmental activities, then we had better be correct about that. It really is putting a level of integrity into the talent assessment process."

Performance Management

Typically, performance management has three components:

- the performance-planning and goal-setting session
- ongoing coaching and feedback between the manager and the MVP against goals, standards, competencies and conformity to company values
- the performance review

The formal identification of talent normally takes place during the performance review session, where the manager and the individual review the accomplishments of the last year. Afterwards, the manager will assign a performance grade, usually from among three options: exceeding expectations, meeting expectations or below expectations. MVPs are those individuals that exceed expectations and consistently outperform their peers in terms of results and adding value to the organization.

Once managers and employees have completed their performance review sessions, data from these sessions is aggregated and rolled up at the team, department, business unit and, finally, corporate levels. The purpose of doing this at the different levels is to ensure that the true talent is identified and the performance ratings are fairly distributed. This is important because development plans and variable pay are dependent on performance ratings.

Not all organizations conduct performance reviews in standard fashion. Seth Wolk, head of global HR for J. Walter Thompson, says that the managers in his organization do not like to fill out forms and grade people, so they have had to create a different process to assess their talent. "We have a performance management system where people get feedback, and we give people reviews. But people in advertising don't like to fill out forms and they don't like to give number grades. They don't want to put people into boxes because that's not the kind of business that we are. Grades are not seen as cool." Instead, Wolk gets the whole management team of an area together. They discuss the performance and potential of individuals and then rate them by consensus as As, Bs and Cs. As Wolk explains, "Although that may seem a simple way to proceed, the fact is that everybody is in agreement, and that is important because they see the person from all different perspectives." They assess people against the following criteria:

- Are they producing incredible work?
- Are they satisfying the client's needs?
- Do they have great potential?

As the J. Walter Thompson experience shows, effective performance reviews need not follow a prescribed formula. Considerable innovation and customization is possible.

Performance management is usually the cornerstone of the talent identification process. It is used at all levels in the organization and is useful in the identification of the "up and coming" talent in the organization. The information from the reviews forms the foundation for talent review.

Talent Review

Typically conducted at more senior levels of the organization, the talent review identifies potential successors to senior leaders and puts in place developmental plans to prepare people singled out for future roles. Attendees for a business unit talent review meeting usually include the heads of departments, the CEO of the business unit and the head of HR for that business. The purpose of a talent review is to:

- share knowledge of the talent across the business unit and the organization as a whole
- identify the MVPs and developmental opportunities for them

The talent review normally evaluates a number of MVPs or potential MVPs by assessing such factors as:

- strengths and weaknesses—typically against competency profiles
- contribution and value to the business unit and company
- development opportunities—needs and recommended actions
- next steps in terms of an individual's interest
- possible next moves

How do actual companies conduct real talent reviews? J. Walter Thompson's process for identifying its stars consists of an annual two-day talent meeting auditing the top 60 positions in the company worldwide. The heads of each country office, the heads of specialist functions and the global head of HR all attend. Their purpose is to identify MVPs and inform them that they have been so identified; to publicize MVP profiles within networks larger than those connected with individual offices; to inform the most senior management of who the company's MVPs are; and to plan for the further development or recruitment of MVPs or potential MVPs. The questions asked at audit sessions include:

- Are there stars in each key position that can help the company achieve its business strategy and potential?

- If there are no stars in a position, what will the company have to do to gets stars? Will it develop individuals to become stars or does it have to recruit them in from outside?

As Seth Wolk says, "It's easy to figure out C players. Even in an extraordinary office or an extraordinary department, where we have an incredible team, the last four people are still your C players. We are constantly thinking about how we get our people better and how we get better people. A lot of what we do at the talent audit meeting on a global basis is to review people, and ultimately take a look at where each person needs to go and then what do we have to do to develop them."

Limited Brands reviews critical talent in its 250 jobs at vice-president level and above many times a year. According to the company's estimate, about 10 percent of those 250 people represent critical talent. There is a review of critical talent in each of the brands, a review of critical talent at enterprise-wide functions such as finance, and finally, a review of all the critical talent at the enterprise-wide level. The senior management team conducts the reviews with their HR business partners at the brands and functional level. Both the Chairman and the Vice Chairman pay a great deal of attention to the talent roll-up process at the enterprise level. The Chairman meets with every CEO and functional head twice a year to do a talent review, and then the Board performs an annual review of critical talent.

Helen Sayles, head of HR for Liberty Mutual, notes that her company has a three-dimensional framework for assessing senior and leadership talent. Management reviews talent against the following dimensions:

- **Capabilities** include the skills and knowledge that people need to have to be successful in the role, such as the ability to focus on the customer, build long-term value, develop people and execute thoroughly.

- **Characteristics** include personal attributes, such as values, traits and management style.

- **Capacity** includes stamina and motivation.

Senior leaders are assessed against these three dimensions and the achievement of their individual goals and the overall business results.

Sayles comments that capabilities can be developed, but the key to defining MVPs is more related to characteristics and capacity. "We believe that you can develop people around the capabilities but you select people around characteristics and capacity. When people fail, particularly at the senior level, it generally does not have anything to do with the capabilities. It generally has to do with some aspect of characteristics and capacity, such as motivation, stamina, values, traits and management style."

She continues, "We find that the MVPs are people with high capacity—high intellectual capacity, high emotional capacity and frankly, high personal stamina. We think that you can build capacity, not by training and normal skill development, but by taking someone out of their traditional comfort zone and putting them into very challenging environments. Over time you are building capacity, you are providing challenge, you are providing that stimulation for the MVP over and over again." Sayles also makes the point that "the responsibility for managing talent in the organization is not mine, nor should it be. It is absolutely an operational management role."

According to Lou de Ocejo and John Marrs, State Street is beginning to put in place an objective process to assess talent at the most senior levels in this global organization. State Street identifies critical positions in the company and then does a full assessment of individual incumbents in those positions. With the aim of discovering people's strengths and areas for development, assessments are based on a 360-degree review against the 16 key competencies identified as crucial to success at senior levels of the organization. Assessments also include testing of analytical and numeric skills, and behavior-based interviews. An outside company does the assessment, and the data from the review is used to compare the senior population against their peers within State Street, and within the financial services sector. This process aims at identifying MVPs at the senior level, and at the next level down in the organization. It also aims at determining the type of development that these MVPs need to become even better.

Lou de Ocejo also tells us about a pilot process that has been implemented in the Global Markets Group. "Over 20 people worldwide were very comprehensively assessed for an entire day, using psychometric tools, structured interviews, behavioral interviews and all kinds of other appropriate tools as a way of determining the current level of talent in the organization, potential talent and how they stack up against the marketplace. Below that top 20 group, we've started to identify potential successors, people with talent—more of the high-potential process."

Sue Lueger, head of HR for Northwestern Mutual, explains that her company has a talent review process to look at both potential successors and up-and-coming talent in the organization. "We have more formal conversations twice a year to review up-and-coming talent in the company. We start with interviewing every single department head to get a view of the potential successors and also to see who else is coming up lower down in the organization that we need to pay attention to." Lueger notes that the managers will often call HR to tell them about a talented person that they have in their department. "The managers will often call us and say that they have a person who looks like they're really talented, and that they would like to get a better handle on what they need to do for them. We might suggest the 360-degree process, or we might have someone from another group conduct a short interview with them over the telephone. Sometimes we gather some objective information on them via assessment tools."

Thus the talent review process typically consists of a series of meetings at various levels of the organization to clearly identify MVPs. The next stage is to put in place the development plans for people that may have been suggested during the course of the reviews.

Development Processes

Some managers are reluctant to identify valuable talent, for fear that they will be taken away from them and thus be unable to contribute to the success of the department. However, an essential component of any development plan involves moving MVPs around so that they acquire the experience necessary to take on increasingly senior roles. The senior management team and the HR function must ensure, therefore, that MVPs are identified, so that they can contribute more to the total organization.

Once MVPs have been identified and confirmed as key talent, the next step is to begin implementing development plans. Developmental planning initiatives ensure that the MVPs are ready to take on assignments that will help the business achieve its strategies and goals. They also provide the challenge and growth that MVPs crave, thereby helping to ensure that they remain committed to staying with the organization. The various ways that MVPs can be developed include:

- encouraging their participation in special projects and assignments
- facilitating planned moves and rotations to expand capabilities and skills
- providing feedback through 360-degree tools and feedback sessions
- inviting MVPs to attend formal talent development sessions

Participation in Special Projects and Assignments

A number of organizations use high-profile project teams and task groups to develop their talented people and to give them broader exposure to the organization.

Helen Sayles of Liberty Mutual explains that her company puts its best talent on project teams. "We develop MVPs by putting them on internal teams that are commissioned from time to time to do process redesign or important project work. Usually those teams are cross-functional in nature, so we enlist high-potential people to get them different work experiences and at the same time give them the opportunity to solve important business issues." Sue Lueger of Northwestern Mutual also talks about giving MVPs more developmental opportunities by leading important projects. "Maybe they've managed day-to-day operations and they've done a great job of coaching and counseling and dealing with their group of employees but they've never had a very high-visibility, important project to manage and lead. You might put them on a team so that they learn that this is how project teams function and get some project management training."

The use of cross-functional teams as a means of development helps the organization to arrive at better business solutions, allows the MVP to learn more about the business and exposes MVPs to a broad range of senior managers who can see their talent firsthand.

Planned Moves and Rotations to Expand Capabilities and Skills

Talent assessment and identification will often identify the need for the MVP to acquire more capabilities and skills. HR and senior management must help develop MVPs, whether by moving them to different functions or by exposing them to progressively more complex management responsibilities. In doing so, however, they must take care not to move MVPs before they have learned enough about the business in their present positions. Moving MVPs too quickly can ultimately cause them to derail because they haven't yet acquired the base skills necessary to succeed. Equally, it is important that MVPs do not stay too long in a role, since they may get overlooked for other opportunities, or get bored and move elsewhere!

The development of MVPs requires moving them around to different functions and making sure that they do something completely different. Sue Lueger notes that during Northwestern Mutual's succession planning process, managers talk about what development action they need to take with people. "Should we rotate this person to another area? What are we expecting them to learn there? For instance, if that person is really great, and they have good potential to manage others, their head is on straight and they can execute and get results. But [if] they haven't managed anybody yet then it is probably time to give them a small group of people to manage."

While the rationale for moving the MVP is clear, acting on that rationale is often a challenge. Megwin Finegan, Senior Partner and Director of Training and Development for J. Walter Thompson, stresses the need to move people despite the clear incentives not to. "There are some agencies where people can be on an account for a very long period of time. That's probably really convenient for the agency, and convenient for the client, but we really believe that our best people are the ones that you can move around. We do it at the right time to make sure that we do not sacrifice continuity for a given client. In fact, to make any placement or any rotation, you have to be right on three dimensions—for the person, for the agency and for the client. To get those stars to line up is so difficult, and that's why we spend a lot of time figuring that out. And I think it's key to keeping MVPs that we give them new experiences at the right moment in time—right for them, right for the business, right for the client." It's often easier to keep the MVP in place, but in the long term moving the MVP is best for the MVP, the organization and even the client.

Some organizations emphasize building jobs around the capabilities of their MVPs, in order to ensure that they receive the right developmental experiences and the right incentives to remain with the company. J. Walter Thompson is clearly such an organization. Seth Wolk, global head of HR, explains, "We often build jobs around MVPs. Megwin [Finegan] has done three or four different kinds of roles, all based on what she does the best, and so her talent has found her job. Same thing with Marc [Capra]. Marc ran an office, Marc ran a region, but now Marc's playing a COO role, dealing with issues of managing people in the creative area."

Deborah Huret, an MVP in J. Walter Thompson's London office, illustrates the importance of building a job for the MVP by relating her own experiences. After joining the company's New York office in 1996, she decided to do her MBA at Harvard in 2000. The company was not only supportive, writing her a letter of recommendation and staying in touch throughout her Harvard studies, it also kept a job open for her. Although a number of companies sought to recruit her once she finished at Harvard, she returned to the company largely because of the skills fit and developmental experiences her new job offered. As worldwide account manager of the Diamond Trading Company, Deborah is now responsible for coordinating the strategy in the 16 markets and offices that cover this account.

Part of the challenge of providing the right development opportunity is to ensure that the MVP works with the right manager. The role of the manager is to ensure that MVPs receive the right challenge and develop the skills that are required for them to progress further. As highlighted in earlier chapters, the manager also needs to be prepared to coach and counsel the individual MVP so that he or she grows and develops. Bob Jeffrey, the CEO, Worldwide of J. Walter Thompson, mentions how important it is to ensure that the MVP is working with the right person. "One of the most important elements of developing an MVP is ensuring that he or she is matched with the right person. It's a failure on the part of the company when you have a really strong MVP who is not working for the right person, and ultimately gets stymied and stifled and wants to go elsewhere. The key is making sure that the MVP is with the right manager who will delegate as much as possible and allow this person to grow."

Not all rotations and planned job moves are successful for either the MVP or the organization. The issue then becomes what to do with the MVP when this happens. A number of organizations suggest that you don't throw the baby out with the bathwater. If MVPs fail in one position, they may be good somewhere else and it is important to give them another chance. Jeffrey talks about a person who seemingly did not have the right skills for the agency, but ended up creating a very different and successful approach for the agency. "There was a guy who was running the Wall Street Journal account and helped win the Merrill Lynch account. I was told that he didn't conform to a lot of the behavior that was expected of account people, and also that he would not become 'the guy' who would run a piece of business. Since I don't believe in typecasting people, and I knew that this young man had many talents, I said that not everybody in an agency is there to be the leader of a big business or the head of a big office. I took him out of the system and used him in a very kamikaze fashion to help with business development. What's interesting is that we're currently developing a new project management discipline in the agency, and this young man is one of the first people who's involved, as his strengths are much better suited to the project management approach. Ironically, we're now developing a system that formalizes something I did spontaneously. We took somebody who was somewhat of a renegade and parlayed that into an advantage for the company."

Feedback Through 360-Degree Tools and Feedback Sessions

An approach being used more widely in organizations is the 360-degree feedback tool and the subsequent feedback sessions. Selected individuals receive feedback against a particular set of competencies. Questionnaires on levels of competencies are typically completed by individuals themselves, their managers, their subordinates and a group of peers. There is usually space for comments on behaviors, skill levels and areas for development. The results of the questionnaires are usually compiled by external firms and a report is created for the individual, who learns of the contents from a skilled facilitator and coach. The contents are usually also shared with the manager. The feedback then becomes the basis for the creation of a development plan by the manager and the individual.

Sue Lueger explains how the results of the 360-degree feedback process have provided learning opportunities at both the individual and departmental level. "The 360 process gets the talent to think about their own development and what they should be focusing and concentrating on. They not only go through the process, but they go back for a feedback session with a developmental person, where they talk through the content of the report plus the suggestions for development." Lueger goes on to describe how the 360-degree process has helped at a departmental level. "Our law department right now is going through a process to determine the role for the department head. All the people in these departmental sessions are talking about such things as needing help from others and giving each other feedback on what happens when I do this well, or how I remember to do such and such. They control all the content of the sessions, and how much they want to share with each other."

Attendance at Formal Talent Development Sessions

More and more organizations are running internal leadership and development programs for their talented people. While these programs have been around in organizations for many years, the new feature is that they consist of a mixture of learning and participation in company-wide project work. Internal leaders act as coaches and counselors to the participants. These programs offer a chance for the participants to learn more about the business, allow them to get to know a broader group of people in the organization and provide them with opportunities for exposure to senior leaders.

These programs also give the heads of the business a chance to get to know their talent better. At the instigation of CEO David Lissy, Bright Horizons Family Solutions developed a leadership development program that enables Lissy to get a better view of this talent. He started this program in order to "find a way to get closer to the people we talk about as our stars. I had a chance to work with a lot of people in my old role, and I always heard a lot about certain people. We wanted to bring ourselves closer to these people." A group of 16 senior management and middle managers who must be sponsored by their supervisors apply to attend a series of two-day meetings that take place four times a year. The meetings consist of some assigned group project work with presentations back to the total group. They also incorporate outside leadership-training resources and include a series of relaxed discussions on defined topics. Lissy pointed to the number of benefits from this program: the participants have exposure to broader strategic discussions than they would have in their specific function; and the senior team is able to assess whether participants are talented people and assess whether they can take on bigger and broader roles. As Lissy notes, "The program provides a chance for us to see some of the talented people and to see which ones possess the capability to go further. We see this in the thoughtfulness of their comments, consideration, questions, just their general conduct in the group. It is very clear. So this has become a great way to touch a certain layer of management."

Sue Lueger of Northwestern Mutual also talks about setting up a leadership group that is aimed at self-development and sharing ideas about the company. This group consists of about 18 people. She explains, "They go through about six months of practice on different topics with a facilitator and coach. They also go through their 360s. The main focus of the group is for them to learn about themselves, learn about how they could manage better, and share ideas with each other."

As reported in *The Wall Street Journal*, Steve Reinemund, chairman and CEO of PepsiCo, has launched an executive leadership program aimed at helping the senior managers know their MVPs and each other better.[1] Designed for high-performing senior middle managers in key jobs, it helps prepare them to become future leaders of the company. The program, which so far has involved about 80 participants, consists of two separate week-long sessions and focuses on personal growth as well

---

[1] Carol Hymowitz, "PepsiCo Chief Executive Asks Future Leaders to Train Like Athletes," *The Wall Street Journal* (September 9, 2003): In The Lead section. inthelead@wsj.com

as business topics such as corporate strategy, ethics, change and innovation. The company directors deliver most of the program, so they and the middle managers can get to know one another better. Some of the training classes are led by a psychologist who believes that executives must train in the same systematic way as professional athletes in order to perform successfully over the long haul. He challenges PepsiCo executives to reflect on their lives and identify something they want to change that will give them more energy and enable them to better motivate subordinates. They may want to become more physically fit, for example, or improve their nutrition or take up meditation to reduce stress.

Reinemund says the training program is helping him get better acquainted with middle managers. "I work with all these people during the course of a year, but this gives me a chance to get to know them much more personally—and get a sense of what people [down the ranks] feel," he says. He thinks the program fosters camaraderie among executives who work in different businesses and locations around the globe, and helps him retain management talent. He stays in touch with participants by holding conference calls with them six months after the end of each session. He also enlists their help on certain special projects. Some of the former participants are contributing to a task force that is compiling a list of corporate values for PepsiCo. Reinemund hopes that, in the end, the leadership program will help managers decide which specific strengths and talents they wish to build up and which new skills they must attempt to acquire.

Megwin Finegan of J. Walter Thompson explains that her company has a professional development program for assistant account executives, and for junior account planners and junior creative people who are generally recruited out of college. She explains that many companies tend to think of MVPs as being senior people because they are the most responsible for the revenue, etc. However, at J. Walter Thompson they believe that MVPs can be identified early on. "This business is a bit of a meritocracy, and good ideas come from anywhere, including our junior people. In this training program we place a lot of emphasis on the final presentation, which is done for senior management and most recently also to clients; because we use a live project, we have a combination of clients and senior management in the room. The final presentation is a big deal. You see people in action and already you've targeted some people. And sure enough, over time they are the ones who consistently prove themselves to be of MVP potential or caliber."

Continental Airlines has a slightly different approach to development. It provides opportunities for people to network and to work in the organization and determine if there is a fit between their career aspirations and the needs of a given department. Mike Campbell, the Senior Vice President, Human Resources and Labor Relations, explains how HR has put in place the processes to allow this to work. "We have in place an organization called the Continental Management Association, which is a group of our managers who've formed an association that provides networking opportunities for people to come to business outings, cocktail parties or lunches to meet people and to cross-divisionally meet people, and to express interests of moving within the company. So we've set up this management association for people to network and to mentor. The other thing is when we from time to time need temporary employees, just like any company, and we set up a program where we encourage managers to let people who can be spared from other divisions go, and we encourage these employees to come over and work in other divisions on a temporary basis, 60 to 90 days, as an opportunity to a) see whether they like working in another division, b) show their talents to those in that division, and then c) put them in a competitive position when there are openings to bid in that division. So we look for people who want to help themselves. HR has helped put processes and opportunities in place for them."

Recruitment to Fill Talent Gaps

In some cases, attempts to identify and develop talent may lead to the realization that MVPs must be brought in from the outside. Although Chapter 6 covered the topic of recruitment of external MVPs and their assimilation into the new organization, we have yet to touch on the specific roles played by HR in MVP recruitment. Those roles include:

- scouting talent
- defining the organization's MVP needs and expectations
- designing compensation and benefit packages
- assisting with MVP assimilation

Scouting Talent

Many organizations like to keep track of the MVPs in their industry and profession. As we noted earlier, MVPs are well-known externally because of the various kinds of value they create in the company and the industry. Increasingly, managers are expecting HR to track the careers and locations of MVPs as preparation for any future recruitment pitch the organization may decide to make. Keeping track of MVPs can mean:

- attending industry and professional meetings that MVPs may speak at or attend, and being present in places where the HR person can network to learn about current and potential "players"
- reading industry and trade magazines and business newspapers to glean ideas on talent
- asking managers to identify MVPs they know of in other organizations and arranging to meet with these MVPs either formally or informally
- keeping names of valuable people previously interviewed but not hired, on the assumption that the company may find a better fit for them at a later date
- using recruitment firms to identify MVPs in the industry

J. Walter Thompson serves as a good example of an organization that tracks external MVPs. Seth Wolk, head of the company's global HR function, keeps an eye on the careers of MVPs and maintains a database so that he knows who he might want to hire in the future. "For instance, we may interview a person for a position as an assistant account executive, but not hire them. But we keep in contact with them, as they become an account executive, account supervisor or account director in another firm. We get to know these people and watch their careers. We put their names into a database that catalogs people by their skills and experiences. That way we keep track of what they are doing."

Wolk also has an interesting perspective on why you want to keep an eye on MVPs. He wants to hire them in order to create value for his firm but equally to ensure that the firm continues to maintain its competitive edge. As he explains, "It's all about having the best talent. It's like a baseball game. And it's an interesting environment because, from a recruiting standpoint, it's a double-edged sword. You want to get a Barry Bonds because he hits home runs for you in the games, but you also want to make sure he doesn't go to the other team in your division because he'll hit home runs for them and you'll lose. So it's all about scouting talent on the outside and, more importantly, scouting and growing talent on the inside."

Defining the Organization's MVP Needs and Expectations

As noted previously, newly recruited MVPs sometimes fail because management isn't always clear on what results it expects the MVP to deliver and on what type of person fits into the organization's culture. The role of HR is to work with managers and key stakeholders to help them clearly define the skills, competencies and past experiences required from MVP recruits. HR must also help formulate a clear description of the type of person that will fit into the organization. Once the job and personality required have been clearly defined, HR must ensure that all interviewers are clear about which questions to ask the MVP and about how the company and its culture is to be portrayed to the candidate. The interviewers have to provide a good experience for the potential candidate, and view it as a public relations and selling exercise. HR should also ensure that the MVP is interviewed by the appropriate influential people. Only then can both the interviewers and the MVP determine if the candidate will suit the organization and fit in with management priorities.

Assessing culture fit may best be conducted in an informal setting. Some organizations will set up lunches or dinners for the MVP so that he or she can meet with potential bosses and peers. Such situations allow for a better assessment of cultural fit, since they give a broader view of cultural dynamics than what emerges in a one-on-one interview. It is also important, as Seth Wolk says, "to meet with people multiple times to try to get a social feel for them, try to get a better understanding, and then just be as realistic about the job as possible."

MVPs and their prospective managers will also need to meet frequently to ensure that the fit and chemistry between them is right. Managers should satisfy themselves that their MVPs will produce the required results, and MVPs should strive to establish a rapport with their managers to circumvent any possibility that managers will feel intimidated by them.

If a candidate is deemed not to be a good fit for a particular position, HR should encourage interviewers to consider the candidate's fitness for another job. An MVP could be hired to do project work until another more appropriate opportunity becomes available in a few months' time. Preventing an MVP candidate from joining another company should also always be a consideration in hiring decisions.

Designing Compensation and Benefit Packages

Another key HR role in MVP recruitment involves working with management to design a competitive compensation and benefit package attractive to the MVP. "Nickeling-and-diming" the MVP at this stage in the process will likely to turn him or her off. One of us vividly remembers being involved in the potential hiring of a well-respected and influential MVP from a global organization. All stages of the recruitment process had gone well and the MVP wanted to join the organization, a subsidiary of a large company. But the pay offer accepted by the MVP, while competitive with the compensation provided by her current employer, was outside the parameters of the compensation usually received by someone in the role she agreed to fill. When the offer was sent to the parent company for review, delays ensued as parent and subsidiary negotiated. In the meantime, the MVP's current organization caught wind of her intentions to leave and made her an offer to join them in another part of the world. She readily agreed. In the end, dithering over compensation cost our client an MVP!

Assisting with MVP Assimilation

The assimilation or on-boarding process for the new MVP was described in detail in Chapter 6. Here we will mention the contributions the HR function should make to this process:

- providing the manager with assimilation resources that either exist in the company or may be acquired from external firms that focus on career development and assimilation of new people
- coaching the newly hired MVP, particularly on the expectations of the organization, the changing needs of stakeholders and the intricacies of adapting to the culture

Recognition and Rewards

As part of its contribution to MVP development, HR has an essential role to play in designing approaches to recognize and reward the MVP, predominantly from a compensation perspective. There are four key elements in a recognition and rewards program: base pay (salary), benefits, variable pay and recognition. Salary and benefits tend to be determined by market forces and the rate for a particular job, together with geographical differentials. Variable pay and recognition are based on the performance of the individual, the team and the company as a whole. The table below shows the types of programs in the four elements.

	Base pay and benefits	**Performance-based rewards**
CASH	**SALARY** • job-based pay • market-based pay • competency-based pay • geographical differentials • merit pay increases	**VARIABLE PAY** • individual variable pay • team variable pay • company profit sharing • stock options/ grants—short and long term
NONCASH	**BENEFITS** • benefits—health and insurance • benefits—retirement • training and education • wellness programs	**RECOGNITION** • promotions • special assignments • professional develop-ment • public/private recogni-tion • informal recognition

This section will focus on variable pay and recognition schemes used for the MVP. However, we should first emphasize the importance of providing MVPs with base pay and benefits at the top of a salary range, or even beyond it in some cases. MVPs should never feel that they are underpaid relative to their peers in the company or in the external market. Their energy needs to be focused on creating value for the company, not on issues of compensation.

As for variable pay for MVPs, many organizations use different types of performance-based incentives that link to both the short-term financial health and the long-term potential of the organization. Seth Wolk of J. Walter Thompson explains that his organization has a variety of variable-pay programs that are based on the performance of the individual and the company. "We have incentives at the more senior level. We also have a variety of incentive programs that are very limited and these have two benefits. Firstly, the value of the potential financial outcome is very important and keeps people with us, and secondly, the awareness that they're getting a scarce resource is great. We only give these limited incentives to motivate our more senior people, and they're all different and based on different levels of performance. We also have a bonus system for individual performance, and we have a rolling three-year incentive that is about company performance. And then people can also get options, based on their contribution to WPP [the parent company] as a whole."

Diane Hessan, the CEO of Communispace, explains how she uses long-term stock options as a way to recognize her MVPs. "We recently gave some options out to people. What I decided to do, rather than give out an even amount of options to everyone, was to give a disproportionate amount of options to value-creating people. I would have a meeting with the top people and say to them that 'the purpose of this meeting is to give you stock options. Let me tell you what these options are and how they work. When you walk out of here I would like you to feel that I drove a truck up to your office and I emptied the thing out into your garage and it was overflowing with options. I want you to feel like you got a truckload. They are not that valuable now, but at some time when the company is valuable I want to make sure that people like you benefit.'"

While generous compensation is important, money alone cannot fully account for the motivations of MVPs. As Hessan tells us, "It's not only about money. True MVPs don't ask for more base pay. When people feel that they are critical, that their voice matters, that they make a difference, and that they're important, they do not pull that bullshit [make salary demands] with you. They walk in and say, 'I matter, I'm important, I'm special, I have a piece of this, and this is so great. It's the biggest part of my compensation package.' It's never about the money. People want to matter. People want to make a difference. People want to feel valued. I've never in my 25 years as a manager had this backfire on me. What does backfire is when somebody comes in and says, 'I'm not making enough money.' I break all the rules; I give them more money and six months later they are gone."

Deborah Huret works in the London office of J. Walter Thompson and also mentions that MVPs do not work solely for the money. They value the contribution they make to their clients and they want the "psychic" recognition for such things as helping the business and the individuals grow and develop. She makes the point that MVPs tend to far outperform their peers and sometimes their managers may simply leave them alone to get on with things. She pointed out that MVPs do need recognition and should not be taken for granted, even if it is only to get a thank you in private.

Bob Jeffrey, CEO, Worldwide of J. Walter Thompson, explains that non-financial rewards in his industry can often be as powerful as salaries and bonuses. However, he does note that financial rewards are important. "You have to think very creatively about how to deal with people on a compensation level. Salary isn't the only thing. We have incentive plans that include stock and options programs. Also, when we hit our annual financial forecasts, we pay out bonuses to eligible employees. It's important that you tie compensation to performance and that people feel like this is a financial recognition of the hard work and commitment that they have demonstrated throughout the year. You also have to have to be psychologically connected to your employees. They have to respect you and the way the company is run. But to say that that's enough is ridiculous, because New York is a very expensive place to live."

Jeffrey tells us when he and a partner had their own agency where employees were given the opportunity to win national awards in the advertising business. "My best friend Gary and I had our own creative agency. We won one award after another, but we never had large salaries to pay people. What I could promise was that young people would have an opportunity to win some awards. Winning a creative award, especially at a young age, is a token to bigger challenges, grander opportunities and exponentially increased salaries. At larger agencies, the young creatives don't often have the opportunity to enter and win the awards. I'm not underestimating the money side, but if you arm these highly energetic young people with opportunities, chances are that they'll stay with the company. Frankly, most people can find opportunities to go somewhere else and make more money. However, most MVPs do not get up in the morning thinking about the money. They think more along the lines of *Field of Dreams*: If you build it, they will come. My mantra is 'Just do it, and the money will follow.'"

A key point in compensating MVPs is to not make the options and bonuses automatically the same from one year to the next. MVPs like the challenge of constantly re-earning their bonuses and options. Gordon Bethune, Chairman and CEO of Continental Airlines, talks about a bonus program he put in place. "One of the first things I put in place in 1995 when we were broke was a bonus program for the top 20 executives. I told the Board to set the financial goals we needed to achieve. I didn't want them annualized. I wanted them set every quarter because people tend to put things off. If we get off to a bad start in February, you think we can catch up in October. I told my team, 'Every three months that you make your numbers, we will pay a quarter of the bonus. But if you miss the first-quarter number, you lose your quarter bonus forever. If you get ahead of it, then it's easier to make the second quarter." Bethune also explains that Continental has a bonus program for middle managers. "We also have a 25 percent bonus—a bonus program for the middle level—which I administer. Fifty percent of the bonus is based on company productivity and 50 percent is based on how you manage your department and reach the goals that were set. Another 25 percent is based on the results of an employee survey, which makes the total bonus possibility 125 percent. If your employees don't give you a high score, you don't get the 25 percent, so guess what you do."

John Marrs of SSgA notes the importance of providing flexibility to the real MVPs in the company. "If we've got a real star who needs something different in terms of flexibility, certainly we are pretty receptive to that. We've had people who really wanted to do an MBA and they didn't have the money to finance the program because they wanted to go to a top-tier school and also take a certain amount of time off. So we substituted an MBA for their bonus; rather than get their bonus, they got to do their MBA. I think generally, when we have an MVP, we will at least be more receptive to doing what we can to accommodate that individual. We will certainly be flexible in how we deliver things to accommodate a top performer." Marrs also notes that higher bonuses and a share in the equity programs gives the MVPs a lot more from a bonus perspective. "If they are very strong performers, we are certainly going to differentiate what they get versus what the average performer gets. We give them more equity to ensure that they stay with us and that they are given a message that they are important to the long-term viability of the organization."

Recognition is not solely about compensation. It can also be linked to winning prestigious awards in the organization. Marc Capra, COO of J. Walter Thompson, describes two recognition programs that have been instituted by the agency to recognize some of the characteristics of MVPs or potential MVPs. The two awards are the Passion and the Full Bright award. The Passion Program has been created to recognize, promote and celebrate the best creative ideas, talent and product throughout the JWT North American network. The program and the awards are aimed at individuals responsible for bringing passion to the process, and taking great ideas and turning them into great advertising. The second program is the Full Bright award, which is given to the 10 people in the organization that have the skill set and attitude that the company values. It is based on three types of brightness:

- a sharpness of mind that produces creative solutions and new ideas naturally
- a physical brightness that fuels others and fuels work
- a brightness of soul in a person that exudes a passion for life, a permanent dissatisfaction with the status quo and a desire to always raise the bar higher

These honors set a high standard for others who view the winners as role models for becoming an MVP.

Variable rewards and recognition programs ensure that the MVPs know that they are valuable to the organization. HR's role in creating such schemes shouldn't be overlooked.

HR Policies

HR is sometimes viewed as having policies that are unable to adapt to the needs of individuals in the organization. Helen Sayles, head of HR for Liberty Mutual, notes that it is often the MVPs themselves who point out that policies are getting in the way. "What tends to happen over time is that people will use the policies in a way that is dysfunctional as opposed to the way they were intended. The key for us is to be able to recognize when they become dysfunctional so that we know when we need to change. The MVPs will be the ones who will be first to say, 'This is really stupid,' 'This is not working, or 'This is having the wrong outcome' as opposed to having blind faith in a policy or process that may have outlived its usefulness." On the other hand, in some organizations the perception of HR policies is changing as heads of HR are becoming more flexible in policy application. Sayles comments, "I think the notion of uniformity in HR policies and procedures has really dissipated. I think the high-performing organizations are going to be able to differentiate ruthlessly. Differentiation is really key."

Certain policies and benefits should be in place to make MVPs' lives easier and to enable MVPs more time to focus on work. For instance, the provision of concierge services for making reservations for dinners and theaters can take pressure off the MVPs when they are working long hours. Temporary childcare and eldercare services are also very helpful in emergencies or when MVPs need to focus their energy on work. So are policies showing sensitivity to the stresses of relocation. A company's actions during such a crucial time in an MVP's life can send important signals to the MVP. To accommodate special family circumstances, it can be helpful to provide telecommuting and flexible working hours. After all, what matters more—work output or face time? It is important to be flexible and generous. Failure to do so can undermine the MVP's sense of being valued and his or her esteem for the company.

HR policies governing the MVP must be flexible and sensitive to the pressures faced by MVPs. Make sure they are not so rigid that they get in the way. Make sure that they support the MVP's work in imaginative ways. Make sure that they fully reflect the MVP's value to the organization.

Summary

This chapter considered the role of HR in relation to the management of MVPs. It covered the following topics:

- talent assessment
- development processes
- recruitment to fill talent gaps
- recognition and rewards
- HR policies

Summary

Our quest in writing this book was to determine whether the concept of the MVP, which exists in every major sport, was relevant to business. Throughout the course of our interviews, we learned that the concept of the Corporate MVP is relevant and easily defined. These MVPs are the 5 percent or so of people in organizations who are highly valued because they generate the highest revenue; drive quality; produce great customer relations; develop new products and services; and increase the reputation of the business. A number of the business leaders that we interviewed metaphorically say that they "would die if these people left the business."

One of our interviewees tells us of the value she created by identifying and focusing on her MVPs. "These are the people that we are always trying to get our best people to develop into; they are right in front of us. They walk around the office every day, exemplifying the very best that this company can be."

A Review of the Findings

Every organization has its unique group of MVPs, and the members of this elite group vary depending on who is creating the list. Some executives highly value those people who can complement their own areas of weakness. A strong and charismatic CEO with whom we spoke quickly identified her Vice President of Operations as an MVP. She knew that as long as he was running the shop she could focus on market trends, product development, talent recruitment and finances. Their mutual trust significantly enhanced her performance. In turn, this VP identified the Senior VP of Sales and Marketing as one of his MVPs because he could rely on him to provide valid product unit projections. The VP knew that he could plan product manufacturing based on these numbers. What we found was that while the specific lists may vary, every executive had a list of MVPs. Even if they had never before thought of the question "Do you have MVPs in this business?", we always received an immediate "Yes" in response. It then took these executives less than 30 seconds to name at least three people on their list. What is consistent among the lists is that MVPs are a combination of leaders, explorers and producers who can succeed and who share their success with others.

The importance of MVPs is tied directly to the extraordinary value and results these individuals bring to an enterprise. They not only produce extraordinary results but they add to the organization in a way that we began to understand as "performance *plus*." This *plus* factor includes their positive participation in the organization as a whole. They are constantly looking for ways to improve products, processes and people. This then attracts and keeps other talented people who are drawn to excellence. MVPs do this without building a sense of personal entitlement. They do build an ethic of listening, of problem solving and of results. When senior executives recognize that MVPs exist within an organization, they can then maximize the MVPs' positive influence, work to retain them and learn from them.

MVPs work hard to build their success. Their extraordinary results do not occur by just doing a job. When they take on a challenge they begin by learning all they can about the expectations and the resources; then they question all the assumptions that they find are the hidden underpinnings of a job description. They build their jobs to use their talents to reach the desired results. They enlist the talents of others to work with them as part of a team, and then build a culture of success within this team. Just doing the job is too small a task for these comprehensive thinkers. *MVPs focus on building value.* Value is a bigger concept than meeting revenue and profit goals, staying within budget, exceeding expectations or even increasing the stock price. These business standards are part of value building but are not sufficient to describe MVPs' definition of value. MVPs build value every day by constantly improving the organization and the people within it. They do not set out to build value; they set out to do the best that they can do for the organization, with the result being that value increases. To MVPs, value is a combination of the financial measures used to determine an organization's worth and the impact of the organization on the people involved. These people include employees, customers, vendors and the communities the organization touches.

It is worth restating the traits and the qualities that we found describe and differentiate MVPs:

- MVPs are motivated by intrinsic passion
- MVPs always want to succeed and do not like to fail
- MVPs show moral courage
- MVPs are committed to the values and vision of the company
- MVPs enhance the company's reputation
- MVPs earn the respect of colleagues

MVPs are a grouping of remarkable people. The people that we call MVPs epitomize the very best within already very good organizations. MVPs are what managers hope many other talented employees will become.

They thrive under great management and can succeed for a time under poor management. Marc Capra, the COO of J. Walter Thompson, New York, speaks for many MVPs when he says that he will not stay in an unsatisfactory job for more than four days, that he will either fix it within two days or leave on the fourth day. MVPs, as great as they are, cannot manage themselves. Managing these MVPs is critical, to both ensure that they stay with the organization and that they continue to produce the extraordinary results that they are known to produce. MVPs do not tolerate poor management and can be very clear about what they need from good management.

If you are a manager of MVPs, you should talk with your MVPs about what works for them and what does not work. We urge you to use Chapter 4, "Managing the MVP," as a resource guide when you are fortunate enough to have an MVP on your team. There are many ideas presented for managing MVPs, but we would emphasize two ideas here: 1) MVPs flourish under management that creates a culture that motivates and supports the MVPs' productivity, and 2) MVPs flourish when provided with meaningful challenges and opportunities to further grow and develop.

Since MVPs are quite remarkable, it is natural for smart executives to want as many as they can get, or maybe to even become an MVP. Can a talented person become an MVP and, if so, can organizations develop MVPs? MVPs have some natural talents that predispose them to high performance in their area of talent. We acknowledge that not everyone has what it takes to become an MVP but that the drive to improve oneself and one's organization does build the capabilities and stature of all who try.

To increase value, MVPs

- produce extraordinary results
- take calculated risks
- take advantage of luck
- accept challenges
- pursue meaningful work
- engage in honest dialogue
- recognize that attitude makes a difference
- learn and grow

These descriptors create an MVP approach to work that, if adopted, will assist a person wanting to become an MVP to reach his or her goal. Also, an executive can consider these descriptors as an MVP development base.

We found that many top executives work hard to become successful at recruiting MVPs to join their organization. They have to ensure that there is a fit between the needs and culture of the organization and the needs and style of the MVP. Success is not always guaranteed. When bringing an MVP in from the outside it is important to remember that great performance and great compensation are baseline issues for MVPs. What interests an MVP after these two issues have been settled is the alignment they feel with the organization and with the person to whom they will report. Alignment, passion, corporate vision, respect for colleagues, challenge and an ethical underpinning that is consistent with their own are the keys to attracting MVPs. Once hired, the MVP needs help to assimilate from his or her direct manager and key resources such as senior leaders in HR. MVPs are different from most employees in many ways but comfort with and respect for colleagues is a shared desire. The manager needs to stay connected to the new MVP at least until good working relationships are created. The manager should also consider that an MVP's reputation may precede him or her and peers may be threatened by the new MVP. In Chapter 6, "Bringing in the MVP from Outside," we presented a set of ideas and tools that managers may find useful when bringing in MVPs and other talented recruits.

MVPs, like all other humans, have issues and problems that may interfere with their work life. At times, MVPs can cause problems and managers must act to resolve these problems while maintaining the MVP as a corporate asset. In Chapter 7, "Managing Difficult MVPs," we recommended that managers begin managing difficult MVPs by taking time to assess the situation and to put together an internal resource team with HR, senior management and other relevant resources, then put together a course of action with contingency plans as well. We strongly recommend that action be taken to conserve a valuable MVP, as we found that "hope" is an ineffective management tool.

We stress that HR plays a key role in recruiting, hiring, performance managing, developing and retaining the MVP. Their key role is to assist with the identification and development of MVPs. HR partners are also a valued resource to the managers of MVPs to help them manage these resources. While managers are responsible for the day-to-day management of MVPs, HR creates and implements the strategic model and processes for managing them. HR also should have or have access to tactical management expertise that a manager can tap into when a critical situation arises.

Excellence Can Be Contagious

The idea of an MVP is consistent with the idea of excellence. In any grouping of people brought together to complete a task or to reach a goal, there will be some people who are more skilled, more talented and more productive than others. These are the "best" and they create value for the entire group. When we first began the work on this book we met some resistance to the idea of identifying MVPs within work groups. The concern was that by identifying someone as "best" we would make the other group members feel less valued, and this would de-motivate these people. We found the exact opposite to be true. Excellence in their midst, embodied by an MVP, provides a great role model who infects the others with his or her passion and drive. MVPs become a source of pride and energy inside and outside of the team. The more MVPs excel, the more the team excels; it becomes an upward spiral of positively reinforced behavior. We urge senior executives, HR executives and managers to identify, acknowledge, manage and challenge your MVPs. You will improve your entire organization.

It was our goal in our interviews to learn from top businesspeople their definition and understanding of MVPs, and we succeeded. What we had not anticipated was the impact these interviews would have on the senior executives and the HR executives themselves. When we went back to these people to check the accuracy of their quotes, we heard from many that "the MVP concept has begun to permeate our business." When we asked what this meant, we heard that these senior executives and HR executives now include MVPs as a category of employees when they are discussing succession planning, high-potential employee development, and resources for organizational restructuring. MVPs have become a class of employees now viewed as a key asset that should be managed as such. This shift in thinking did not necessitate a reallocation of resources to support MVPs, but rather an inclusion of MVPs as a key resource. The leaders within these organizations are beginning to consider the opportunities and the challenges that they can use to excite their MVP resources, while at the same time resolving real-time business issues. This has included having creative MVPs sit in on financial management meetings, MVP service professionals participating in HR planning, and having operations MVPs participating in product development. They have also been exposing their high-potential people to these MVPs, often cross-functionally, to take advantage of the MVPs' vision, passions and their excellence at employee development. The MVPs are proving to be effective and flexible mentors for developing talent and for instilling passion and moral courage.

The ongoing application by business leaders of MVP thinking has exceeded our original goals for the development of this book. It is our hope that you will incorporate the thinking that the business professionals shared during the interviews, as well as our cross-business perspective, summarized here, to impact your own business management.

We invite you to post your own MVP insights and stories, and read those of others, at www.corporatemvp.com.

꿘

Participating Companies and the People Interviewed

The Companies

The following companies and individuals were interviewed and provided us with the material on which the book is based.

American Distributed Generation

*American*DG supplies low-cost energy to its customers through distributed power generating systems using cogeneration, which is also known as combined heat and power (CHP) technology. The company is committed to providing commercial and small industrial facilities with clean, reliable power and hot water at lower costs than local utilities can supply—without any capital or start-up costs to the energy user. *American*DG is headquartered in Waltham, Massachusetts. For more company information, visit www.americandg.com.

John Hatsopoulos is Vice Chairman of the Board, Chief Financial Officer of *American*DG and a private investor. Mr. Hatsopoulos is also Chief Executive Officer of Tecogen Inc., a DG equipment manufacturer based in Waltham, Massachusetts, and is also Managing Partner of GlenRose Capital LLC, a leverage buyout fund, and Alexandros Partners

LLC, a financial advisory firm. Mr. Hatsopoulos is a co-founder of Thermo Electron Corporation, and the retired President and Vice Chairman of the Board of that company.

Bright Horizons Family Solutions

Bright Horizons is the world's leading provider of employer-sponsored child care and early education, managing more than 500 early care and education centers in the United States, Europe and Canada. Bright Horizons serves more than 400 clients, including 84 *Fortune* 500 companies and 50 of the "100 Best Companies for Working Mothers," as recognized by *Working Mother* magazine. Bright Horizons is one of *Fortune* magazine's "100 Best Companies to Work for in America." The company employs 15,000 people. For or more company information, visit www.brighthorizons.com.

Roger Brown, Executive Chairman and Founder
David Lissy, Chief Executive Officer
Mary Ann Tocio, President, Chief Operating Officer and Director
Ann Pickens, Vice President, Strategic Planning

Communispace Corporation

Communispace is a marketing technology firm that helps companies get deeply connected to their customers and employees. In its most popular application, Communispace creates private, branded "communities" that become virtual customer advisory boards—generating ongoing and action-able insights and increased customer loyalty in record time, with lower costs than traditional methods. It employs 40 people. For more company information, visit www.communispace.com.

Diane Hessan, President and Chief Executive Officer

Continental Airlines

Continental Airlines is the world's seventh-largest airline, with 2,200 daily departures to 127 domestic and 96 international destinations. Continental has the broadest global route network of any U.S. airline, including extensive service throughout the Americas, Europe and Asia. Continental has hubs serving New York, Houston, Cleveland and Guam, and carries approximately 41 million passengers per year. With 42,000 employees, Continental is one of the 100 Best Companies to Work for in America. In 2003, *Fortune* ranked Continental highest among major U.S. carriers in the quality of its service and products, and number two on its list of Most Admired Global Airlines. For more company information, visit www.continental.com.

Gordon Bethune, Chairman and Chief Executive Officer
Larry Kellner, President and Chief Operating Officer
Michael Campbell, Senior Vice President, Human Resources and Labor Relations
Ned Walker, Senior Vice President, Worldwide Corporate Communications

FiRE + iCE Restaurant Chain

FiRE + iCE, an "improvisational grill," opened in Cambridge's Harvard Square in September 1997 and quickly became a favorite with students, office workers, couples and families. Jim Miller, Chief Executive Officer and Founder of FiRE + iCE, expanded his concept opening locations in Providence, Rhode Island in August 1999 and Boston's Back Bay in July 2000. He recently signed a multiunit franchise agreement with Marriott International. Containing a marketplace of fresh meats, seafood, pastas, internationally influenced sauces, and both exotic and traditional vegetables; FiRE + iCE offers diners an endless array of culinary possibilities waiting to be fired up at the 35´ round open grill in the center of the restaurant. The concept has won numerous national awards and "Best of..." ratings in every city in which it is located. It employs a staff of 200+ people. For more company information, visit www.fire-ice.com.

Jim Miller, Founder and CEO.
Keith Brown, Chief Operating Officer

GeneXP Biosciences

GeneXP Biosciences produces robust tools and services that merge automation, biology and informatics to deliver high throughput gene expression analysis to life sciences companies. GeneXP delivers end-to-end solutions and outsourced services for gene expression profiling in high throughput formats—from RNA preparation to hybridization to data analysis. GeneXP Biosciences enables researchers to achieve 5× to 30× improvements in the time and cost of conducting gene expression experiments. The company employs 10 people. For more company information, visit www.genexpbiosciences.com.

Michael Cohen, President

Honeywell International

Honeywell International is a diversified technology and manufacturing leader based in Morris Township, New Jersey. The company serves customers worldwide with aerospace products and services; control technologies for buildings, homes and industry; automotive products; turbochargers; specialty chemicals; fibers; and electronic and advanced materials. The company employs 100,000 in over 100 countries. For more company information, visit www.honeywell.com.

Mark Howes, Vice President, Mechanical Systems & Accessories

Note: The views expressed by Mark Howes represent his personal opinions and not necessarily those of Honeywell.

Humphrey Enterprises, LLC

Humphrey Enterprises, LLC is a private equity investment firm focused on three primary industry sectors: automotive, health care, and training and education. Humphrey Enterprises invests in companies where there is potential for sustainable growth and where the company can secure market-leading positions. The company looks for opportunities where it can invest capital as well as strategic and operational expertise.

John Humphrey, President/Retired Chairman of The Forum Corporation

J. Walter Thompson

J. Walter Thompson (JWT) ranks as the fourth-largest advertising agency brand in the world and the largest in the United States. Its strength is rooted in a global network of 311 offices in 90 countries with over 8,000 entrepreneurial professionals attuned to local culture and dedicated to delivering inventive ideas across borders. A full-service brand communications company, JWT offers its clients integrated marketing solutions across all communications channels. With a strong heritage of innovation—which has been evolving since 1864—JWT is skilled in unlocking the power of brands through "Big Ideas That Work." For more company information, visit www.jwt-world.com.

Bob Jeffrey, Chief Executive Office
Marc Capra, Chief Operating Officer
Kevin Wassong, CEO, digital@jwt North America
Ed Evangelista, Executive Vice President, Executive Creative Director
Seth Wolk, Senior Partner, Director of Human Resources Worldwide
Samantha Digennaro, Senior Partner, Director of Communications
Megwin Finegan, Senior Partner, Director of Training & Development

Deborah Huret, World Wide Account Director
Amanda Feve, Brand Planner

Liberty Mutual Insurance

One of the largest property and casualty insurers in the U.S., Liberty Mutual has over 900 offices in the U.S., Argentina, Australia, Bermuda, Brazil, Canada, China, Colombia, Hong Kong, Ireland, Portugal, Singapore, Spain, Thailand, the U.K. and Venezuela. It employs over 35,000 people. For more information, visit www.libertymutual.com.

Helen Sayles, Senior Vice President, Human Resources and Administration

Limited Brands

Formerly The Limited, the company operates about 4,600 stores in the U.S. Its apparel segment includes The Limited, Express, Henri Bendel, and Structure (rebranded as Express Men's). The intimate brands segment, which accounts for more than half of the company's revenue, is known for its Victoria's Secret (lingerie stores and catalogs), Bath & Body Works (personal care product stores) and White Barn Candle Co. (candles and fragrances). The company also owns apparel maker, Mast Industries. It employs 98,900 people. For more company information, visit www.limitedbrands.com.

Sandy West, Executive Vice President, Human Resources

We also interviewed the President and CEO of a personal care division of Limited Brands, Intimate Beauty Corporation. Intimate Beauty Corporation includes the development and retailing of the Victoria's Secret Beauty line of cosmetics, fragrances and other beauty products. Victoria's Secret Beauty is sold in about 500 Victoria's Secret Beauty retail stores, as well as more than 500 of the Victoria's Secret lingerie stores, the Victoria's Secret Web site and Victoria's Secret catalogs. Intimate Beauty also runs about 10 mall-based aura science stores—part of a joint venture with Shiseido launched in 2002—that offer the aura science brand of cosmetics and skin care products.

Robin Burns, President and Chief Executive Officer of Intimate Beauty Corporation, Victoria's Secret Beauty and aura science

Massachusetts Institute of Technology (MIT)

A leading research institution, MIT is granted more patents annually than any other university, and 55 people associated with MIT are Nobel Prize recipients. Blending that science and engineering acumen with a top business program, MIT graduates have started more than 4,000 companies—Campbell Soup, Hewlett-Packard and Intel, to name just a few. Tuition for MIT's more than 10,000 students runs about US$28,000 a year. The faculty of the 27 academic departments includes over 960 professors. Founded in 1865, MIT is privately endowed. For more information, visit http://web.mit.edu.

Laura Avakian, Vice President of Human Resources
Samuel Jay Keyser, Emeritus Professor of Linguistics, Special Assistant to the Chancellor; Author

MIT Sloan School of Management

Founded in 1914, the management school at Massachusetts Institute of Technology first offered a curriculum in engineering administration. The scope and depth of this educational focus have grown steadily in response to advances in the theory and practice of management to today's broad-based management school. A program offering a master's degree in management was established in 1925. The world's first university-based executive education program—the Sloan Fellows—was created in 1931 under the sponsorship of Alfred P. Sloan, Jr., the 1895 MIT graduate who was then chairman of General Motors. A Sloan Foundation grant established the MIT School of Industrial Management in 1952 charged with educating the "ideal manager." In October 2002, the School celebrated the 50th anniversary of its founding. Today, MIT Sloan is one of the world's leading innovators in management research and practices. For more information, visit http://mitsloan.mit.edu.

Thomas Kochan, George Maverick Bunker Professor of Management

Mintz Levin Cohn Ferris Glovsky and Popeo P.C.

Mintz Levin Cohn Ferris Glovsky and Popeo is a versatile law firm of more than 450 highly qualified and dedicated attorneys representing a diverse international clientele in many industries, who turn to the firm for a wide range of legal services and resources. The firm's clients include major public corporations, privately held and family businesses, entrepreneurs, start-ups and emerging growth companies, investors, underwriters, directors and officers, research scientists, medical and academic institutions, public agencies and industry associations.

Mintz Levin maintains offices in Boston, Washington, Reston, New York, New Haven, Los Angeles and London. For more company information, visit www.mintz.com.

Irwin Heller, Partner and Former Managing Partner

Northwestern Mutual Life Insurance Company

Northwestern Mutual, its subsidiaries and its affiliates offer insurance, investment products and advisory services that address client needs for financial protection, capital accumulation, estate preservation and distribution of estate assets. Products and services for the personal, business, estate and pension markets include permanent and term life insurance, disability income insurance, long-term care insurance, annuities, trust services, mutual funds and other securities. For more company information, visit www.northwesternmutual.com.

Barbara Piehler, Senior Vice President and Chief Information Officer
Susan Lueger, Vice President, Human Resources
John Kordsmeier, Vice President—Underwriting Standards
Barbara Bras, Director of Employee Development
Jeanne Marx, Organization Development Consultant

Novations/J. Howard & Associates

Novations/J. Howard is a multicultural team of management and training experts that specializes in maximizing the performance of all employees in the workplace. Its trainers combine their visible commitment to the principles of development with excellent training skills, a sound business sense and a thorough understanding of the current issues that face professionals in corporate America. Since its founding in 1977, Novations/J. Howard & Associates has been applying theories based in social psychology and human development to attain measurable improvements in performance. Today, the company has 86 employees and conducts business in the United States, Canada, the United Kingdom, Sweden, Chile and Mexico. For more company information, visit www.novations.com.

Mike Hyter, President and CEO
Audra Bohannon, Senior Vice President, Education Services
Gerry Lupacchino, Vice President, Sales and Marketing
Naomi Sutherland, Vice President, Operations and Strategy

NSTAR

NSTAR's power utilities (Boston Edison, Cambridge Electric Light and Commonwealth Electric), which operate as NSTAR Electric, serve customers in about 80 Massachusetts communities, including Boston. Subsidiary NSTAR Gas is present in about 50 communities in central and eastern Massachusetts. It employs 3,300 people. For more company information, visit www.nstaronline.com.

Timothy Manning, Senior Vice President, Human Resources

Phoenix Investments Partners, Ltd.

Phoenix Investment Partners provides asset management services to corporate and individual clients. Operating through about a dozen subsidiaries and affiliates, the company offers access to such investment products as wrap fee programs, closed-end funds and managed account services marketed to wealthy individuals. It administers about 40 open-end mutual funds, as well. Phoenix Investment Partners also provides institutional investment management services to endowments, insurance companies and multi-employer retirement funds. The company has more than US$50 billion of assets under management. The Phoenix Companies, formerly Phoenix Home Life Mutual Insurance, owns Phoenix Investment Partners. For more company information, visit www.phoenixinvestments.com.

Daniel T. Geraci, President and Chief Executive Officer

Pioneer Investment Management, Inc.

Pioneer Global Asset Management S.p.A., including its U.S. subsidiary Pioneer Investment Management, Inc., manages over US$130 billion (as of September 30, 2003) under the name Pioneer Investments®, with over US$29 billion for the U.S. Pioneer's flagship fund, Pioneer Fund. The fund was founded in 1928 and is the fourth-oldest mutual fund in the United States. Pioneer Investments is owned by UniCredito Italiano S.p.A., which is one of Italy's largest banks. The U.S. subsidiary employs approximately 600 people. For more company information, visit www.pioneerfunds.com.

Osbert Hood, Chief Executive Officer
Bill O'Grady, Executive Vice President of Distribution and Sales
John Carey, Executive Vice President, Director of U.S. Portfolio Management and Pioneer Fund Portfolio Manager

Royal Bank of Canada (RBC) Capital Markets

RBC Capital Markets is the corporate and investment banking arm of RBC Financial Group, the global brand for Royal Bank of Canada. RBC Capital Markets is Canada's leading underwriter of debt and equity securities and ranks among the top 10 merger and acquisition advisors in North America. It offers institutional clients a global reach in selected products and industry sectors with a strong focus on U.S. mid-market companies. Royal Bank of Canada is a leading diversified financial services company in North America with over 60,000 employees and 12 million clients through offices in some 30 countries worldwide, and is Canada's largest financial institution as measured by market capitalization and total assets. For more company information, visit www.rbccm.com.

Ian Hendry, Managing Director, HR

Seed Partners, LLC and Growth Point Ventures, LLC

Seed Partners is a hands-on, seed-stage and early-stage private equity firm founded in 1998. It typically invests at a relatively early stage in a company's development and prefers to take on significant hands-on roles—in some cases as interim operating executives. Its investment focus is on advanced engineered products and systems that solve real problems. Growth Point Ventures LLC is a new investment fund created by Seed Partners. For more information, visit www.seedpartners.com and www.growthpointventures.com.

Daniel Behr, Managing Director

Shoppers Drug Mart

Shoppers Drug Mart/Pharmaprix is Canada's largest retail drug store group and is one of the most recognized and trusted names in Canadian retailing. The company's over 844 licensed drug stores and 46 Shoppers Home Health Care stores are situated in prime locations in every province and two territories, making the company one of the most convenient retailers in Canada.

The company was founded in 1962 by Toronto pharmacist Murray Koffler, who believed that it was possible to build a national organization of pharmacies without sacrificing the personalized service of the local community pharmacist. This vision is the cornerstone of the Shoppers Drug Mart/Pharmaprix Associate Concept and has helped build a brand that is synonymous with exceptional service and value. Each Shoppers Drug Mart/Pharmaprix store is owned and operated by a pharmacist-Associate, instilling a strong sense of pride, accountability and community spirit at each location.

Over its 40-year history, the company has grown to become the leading player in Canada's retail drug store marketplace and the number one provider of pharmacy products and services. In fiscal 2002, Shoppers Drug Mart/Pharmaprix stores recorded system sales in excess of C$5.4 billion. It employs 32,000 people. For more company information, visit www.shoppersdrugmart.ca.

Andrew Faas, Executive Vice President, Corporate Development and Human Resources

State Street Corporation

With more than US$8.5 trillion in assets under custody and in excess of US$1 trillion under management, State Street Corporation is a world leader in financial services. The company provides an unwavering client focus with in-depth experience and leading-edge technology to offer an unrivaled breadth of products and services to the global investment community.

State Street's clients are among the most sophisticated institutional and individual investors in the world—investment managers, pension plan sponsors, collective investment fund managers, banks, corporations, not-for-profit organizations and high-net-worth individuals. The company employs 19,000 people globally. For more company information, visit www.statestreet.com.

Luis de Ocejo, Executive Vice President, Human Resources & Organizational Performance
Stanley Shelton, Managing Director and Executive Vice President, State Street Global Markets
Nicholas Bonn, Managing Director and Executive Vice President, Securities Trading
Mark Snyder, Managing Director, Executive Vice President, FX and Money Markets
Simon Wilson-Taylor, Managing Director and Senior Vice President, Global Link

State Street Global Advisors (SSgA)

State Street Global Advisors is the investment management arm of State Street Corporation. An industry leader with over US$1 trillion in assets under management, SSgA's focus is on delivering investment strategies and integrated solutions to institutional and individual investors worldwide. As one of the world's largest investment managers, SSgA has established a global presence with 31 offices and 9 investment centers. Its clients depend on the company to provide sophisticated, customized investment solutions backed by the experience and technology to help them succeed in today's challenging investment environment. For more company information, visit www.ssga.com.

Tim Harbert, Chairman and Chief Executive Officer
Ned Riley, Chief Investment Strategist
John Marrs, Senior Vice President of Human Resources

Executive Recruitment Firms

We also interviewed senior members of two executive recruitment firms, in order to determine the characteristics of MVPs and reasons why they may leave their current organizations.

Jerry Bliley,Vice Chairman, Canada of Spencer Stuart

Spencer Stuart is the foremost privately held, global executive search firm, spanning over 50 offices in 25 countries. Since 1956, the firm has provided select clients with a range of human capital solutions, including senior-level executive search, board director appointments, strategic leadership services and middle management recruiting. Spencer Stuart conducts over 3,000 assignments each year, partnering effectively with clients ranging from the *Fortune* 500, to mid-cap, to emerging growth companies across a broad range of industries and sectors.

Virginia Murray, Vice President, Managing Director, Toronto of A.T. Kearney Executive Search

Established in 1946, A.T. Kearney Executive Search is one of the leading multinational retained search firms, serving clients through a network of 30 offices in 17 countries. The firm is a division of A.T. Kearney, a global, high value-added management consulting firm. A.T. Kearney is the only major firm in the world that combines executive search with strategic management consulting.

Others Who Gave Us Valuable Thinking and Advice on the Identification and Management of MVPs

Peter Benzie is a senior executive in the financial services industry.

Geoffrey S. Ginsburg M.D., Ph.D., Vice President, Millennium Pharmaceuticals, Inc. is a colleague in the pharmaceutical industry.

Kathy McGirr is a former colleague from the financial services sector.

Mimi McGrath, is Vice President of the Boston office of Manchester-MPS Group—a career management consulting firm.

Sherif Nada is the former President of Fidelity Institutional Brokerage Group and is now an investor.

Professor Ed Schein is the Sloan Fellows Professor of Management Emeritus at the MIT Sloan School of Management. He is also one of the founders of organization development and has extensive experience in consulting on organization issues in numerous large and well-known companies.

Anne Hawley Stevens is Managing Partner of ClearRock Inc. (www.clearrock.com), which provides executive and career development services.

Ruth Wright is a Senior Researcher at the Conference Board of Canada. The Conference Board of Canada is the foremost independent, not-for-profit applied research organization in Canada. It helps build leadership capacity for a better Canada by creating and sharing insights on economic trends, public policy issues and organizational performance.

We are also grateful to a number of people who gave us assistance in setting up the interviews and in providing us with material about the various organizations in our sample:

- Danny Goldstein, Public Relations Manager, J. Walter Thompson
- Lynn Heimbruch, Customer Affinity Consultant, Northwestern Mutual
- Nancy Lague, Assistant to the Chairman at Bright Horizons/Family Solutions
- Erica Roy, Manager, Employee Communications at Continental Airlines

卍

Your MVP Potential

W e recommend that you complete the MVP Assessment tool at www.corporatemvp.com to receive a complete score and to use the most updated version.

卍

We have taken the MVP attributes that our interviewees helped us to identify and have expanded them into a questionnaire that can help you to identify where you are strong and where you are weak.

The www.corporatemvp.com questionnaire comes in two forms. One form is worded so that you can enter your own scores for your profile; the second form is worded so that others can answer the questions for a comparison profile. This will allow you to compare your profile with the views of others. The questionnaires automatically self-score and provide interpretation information. There is a small fee for using the on-line instrument.

A simple paper version of "Your MVP Potential" follows:

Your MVP Potential

General Instructions: The purpose of this instrument is to help you to learn your MVP attributes. There are 60 statements below, each describing an attribute of an MVP. Read each statement and determine your strength with each attribute. For each attribute you will decide if you 1) display it often, 2) rely on it when needed or 3) display it at times but cannot really rely on it. **It is in your interest to be as honest with yourself as you can be**. Once you have completed your ranking, you will then add up the number of marks in each column. Your goal will be to have 20 marks in each column. If you do not have 20 in each column, which is likely, then you should review your rankings and move some "borderline" marks to balance the list.

We suggest that you use a pencil.

Instructions:

1) Read each attribute and decide if it is a **1st-tier** attribute (this would be a primary attribute that you display often); **2nd-tier** attribute (an attribute that you can rely on when needed); or **3rd-tier** attribute (an attribute that you may display at certain times but that you cannot really rely on).

2) Now put a mark to indicate its reliability in **only one** of the three columns to the right of each attribute.

3) Finally, you must have **20** marks in each column. Review each statement of attributes and re-score the statements until you have the correct count in each column.

4) When you have completed rating each item and balancing each column to 20, you can follow the last instructions at the bottom of the columns.

	Attributes	A **3rd-Tier** **Attribute**	A **2nd-Tier** **Attribute**	A **1st-Tier** **Attribute**	✓
1	When given a project, I successfully complete it on time and at or above the results required.	Less reliable	Reliable	Strong	
2	My boss expects me to take the lead.	Less reliable	Reliable	Strong	
3	When I see something that needs to be done, I do it.	Less reliable	Reliable	Strong	
4	My performance reviews indicate that I exceed expectations.	Less reliable	Reliable	Strong	
5	I will "rock the boat" if it means producing better results.	Less reliable	Reliable	Strong	
6	I find that I can persuade others to try new things.	Less reliable	Reliable	Strong	
7	When I try something new it often improves what we do.	Less reliable	Reliable	Strong	
8	When I try something new and it doesn't work out, I know that I have gained valuable information.	Less reliable	Reliable	Strong	

	Attributes	A 3rd-Tier Attribute	A 2nd-Tier Attribute	A 1st-Tier Attribute	✓
9	I know that trying a new idea may result in embarrassing myself.	Less reliable	Reliable	Strong	
10	I find interesting opportunities that can improve our business.	Less reliable	Reliable	Strong	
11	Co-workers are intrigued with the opportunities that I identify.	Less reliable	Reliable	Strong	
12	I provide leadership in my area.	Less reliable	Reliable	Strong	
13	I believe that ambiguity opens possibilities.	Less reliable	Reliable	Strong	
14	I am committed to my success.	Less reliable	Reliable	Strong	
15	I am committed to my organization's success.	Less reliable	Reliable	Strong	
16	I work hard *and* I regularly make time for other important aspects of my life.	Less reliable	Reliable	Strong	
17	While work is important, I make time for my family and for myself.	Less reliable	Reliable	Strong	

	Attributes	**A 3rd-Tier Attribute**	**A 2nd-Tier Attribute**	**A 1st-Tier Attribute**	✓
18	I am aligned with my organization's values and vision.	Less reliable	Reliable	Strong	
19	It is important to me that I am aligned with my organization's values and vision.	Less reliable	Reliable	Strong	
20	My organization values what I do.	Less reliable	Reliable	Strong	
21	I enjoy working as part of a great team.	Less reliable	Reliable	Strong	
22	I do not need to lead every team that I am on.	Less reliable	Reliable	Strong	
23	People seek out my thinking on their work.	Less reliable	Reliable	Strong	
24	I represent the company well, both internally and externally.	Less reliable	Reliable	Strong	
25	I am respected by my peers and by senior management.	Less reliable	Reliable	Strong	
26	I project my commit-ment to the success of our venture.	Less reliable	Reliable	Strong	

	Attributes	A 3rd-Tier Attribute	A 2nd-Tier Attribute	A 1st-Tier Attribute	✓
27	I function well as a member of a team.	Less reliable	Reliable	Strong	
28	I put people at ease.	Less reliable	Reliable	Strong	
29	I am trusted.	Less reliable	Reliable	Strong	
30	People like to work with me; they seek me out.	Less reliable	Reliable	Strong	
31	I am willing to take risks, to push the existing methods to make improvements.	Less reliable	Reliable	Strong	
32	I can succeed anywhere in the organization.	Less reliable	Reliable	Strong	
33	I display dedication, confidence, a passion for my job and a sense of urgency.	Less reliable	Reliable	Strong	
34	I am flexible when obstacles surface.	Less reliable	Reliable	Strong	
35	I am a creative thinker.	Less reliable	Reliable	Strong	
36	I am critical thinker.	Less reliable	Reliable	Strong	
37	I am good at helping others succeed.	Less reliable	Reliable	Strong	

	Attributes	A 3rd-Tier Attribute	A 2nd-Tier Attribute	A 1st-Tier Attribute	✓
38	When faced with a problem, I can make decisions.	Less reliable	Reliable	Strong	
39	I make decisions and I can enforce them when needed.	Less reliable	Reliable	Strong	
40	I will decide and act on less than complete information.	Less reliable	Reliable	Strong	
41	I know what is right and wrong when I am faced with a dilemma.	Less reliable	Reliable	Strong	
42	I make decisions based on clear criteria.	Less reliable	Reliable	Strong	
43	I respond well in a crisis.	Less reliable	Reliable	Strong	
44	I have the expertise needed for my role.	Less reliable	Reliable	Strong	
45	I seek out the expertise of others.	Less reliable	Reliable	Strong	
46	I am happy to include the thinking of others whose expertise is greater than mine.	Less reliable	Reliable	Strong	

	Attributes	A 3rd-Tier Attribute	A 2nd-Tier Attribute	A 1st-Tier Attribute	✓
47	I find that others follow my lead.	Less reliable	Reliable	Strong	
48	I know how to do my job.	Less reliable	Reliable	Strong	
49	I know when I need help and I get it.	Less reliable	Reliable	Strong	
50	I perform my defined role very well.	Less reliable	Reliable	Strong	
51	I create value for my team, for my department, for my organization or for my profession.	Less reliable	Reliable	Strong	
52	I manage people well.	Less reliable	Reliable	Strong	
53	I am good at developing the people on my team.	Less reliable	Reliable	Strong	
54	I am seen as someone who helps others succeed.	Less reliable	Reliable	Strong	
55	I can make my ideas operational.	Less reliable	Reliable	Strong	
56	I find that others value what I do.	Less reliable	Reliable	Strong	

	Attributes	A **3rd-Tier** **Attribute**	A **2nd-Tier** **Attribute**	A **1st-Tier** **Attribute**	✓
57	I prefer work that requires me to learn new skills and/or ideas.	Less reliable	Reliable	Strong	
58	I like challenges.	Less reliable	Reliable	Strong	
59	I prefer to work on new tasks.	Less reliable	Reliable	Strong	
60	I relish taking on a challenge that requires me to learn new skills.	Less reliable	Reliable	Strong	
	Number of marks in each column should equal 20	20	20	20	

Review each of your "strong" or 1st-tier attributes and decide which are your 10 most reliable (top 10) MVP attributes. Put a check in the column to the right of each selection.

Review each of your "less reliable" or 3rd-tier attributes and decide which are your 10 least reliable (bottom 10) MVP attributes. Put a check in the column to the right of each selection.

Questions That You Can Ask of Yourself Regarding Your MVP Potential

1) Consider the job that you are in or the job that you want. Which of the attributes would this job require?

2) Do your strong attributes match the job's requirements?

3) Considering the two questions above, which reliable attributes can you develop to improve your likelihood of success?

Rely on Your Strong Attributes and Build Your Selected Less Reliable Attributes

Strong Attributes: You can and do rely on your strengths. These attributes have been both learned and come naturally. It is likely that you rely on your top 10 attributes regularly. You may consider using other not-so-strong attributes more often to build strength in those areas.

Reliable Attributes: These attributes are resources that you often use. When needed you can improve specific attributes with some regular practice.

Less Reliable Attributes: These attributes are likely to cause you some problems. Avoid jobs that rely heavily on them. Find ways to change the job needs and/or find ways to strengthen these less reliable attributes.

Using the Perceptions of Others to Help You to Improve Your MVP Performance

The following Corporate MVP assessment form is for the use of the *purchaser* of this book to use to compare his or her MVP Potential profile with the profile of others (*cohorts*) whose opinions are valued by the purchaser.

It is recommended that the purchaser request one to three peers or managers complete this assessment profile. The people asked to complete this profile should have been in a recent, close working relationship with the purchaser for at least six months.

Once this assessment profile has been completed, the purchaser of this book can compare his or her self-completed profile with the other profiles to see how consistent or inconsistent their self-perception is with the cohort group.

The purchaser of this book may make *up to three paper copies* of the "Your Colleague's MVP Potential" assessment form.

Corporate MVPs, Copyright 2004

Your Colleague's MVP Potential

General Instructions: The purpose of this instrument is to help your colleague (Name_____) to compare his or her current attributes to those of MVPs.

There are 60 statements below, each describing an attribute of an MVP. You will be asked to read each statement and determine your colleague's strength with each attribute based on your knowledge of this person. (To avoid a flurry of "he/she" usage, we refer to "he" throughout.)

For each attribute you will decide if he 1) displays it often, 2) relies on it when needed or 3) displays it at times but it is not a reliable attribute. Once you have completed your ranking, add up the number of marks in each column. Your goal will be to have 20 marks in each column. If you do not have 20 in each column, which is likely, then you should review your rankings and move some "borderline" marks to balance the list.

We suggest that you use a pencil.

Instructions:

1) Read each attribute and decide if it is a **1st-tier** attribute (this would be a primary attribute that he displays often); **2nd-tier** attribute (an attribute that he can rely on when needed); or **3rd-tier** attribute (an attribute that he may display at times but it is not a reliable attribute).

2) Now put at mark to indicate its reliability in **only one** of the three columns to the right of each attribute.

3) Finally, you must have **20** marks in each column. Review each statement of attributes and re-score the statements until you have the correct count in each column.

4) When you have completed rating each item and balancing each column to 20, return your completed form to the individual who asked you to complete it.

	Attributes	A 3rd-Tier Attribute	A 2nd-Tier Attribute	A 1st-Tier Attribute	✓
1	When given a project, he successfully completes it on time and at or above the results required.	Less reliable	Reliable	Strong	
2	His boss expects him to take the lead.	Less reliable	Reliable	Strong	
3	When he sees something that needs to be done, he does it.	Less reliable	Reliable	Strong	
4	I believe that his performance reviews indicate that he exceeds expectations.	Less reliable	Reliable	Strong	
5	He will "rock the boat" if it means producing better results.	Less reliable	Reliable	Strong	
6	He finds that he can persuade others to try new things.	Less reliable	Reliable	Strong	
7	When he tries something new it often improves what we do.	Less reliable	Reliable	Strong	
8	When he tries something new and it doesn't work out, he knows that he has gained valuable information.	Less reliable	Reliable	Strong	

	Attributes	A 3rd-Tier Attribute	A 2nd-Tier Attribute	A 1st-Tier Attribute	✓
9	He knows that trying a new idea may result in embarrassing himself.	Less reliable	Reliable	Strong	
10	He finds interesting opportunities that can improve our business.	Less reliable	Reliable	Strong	
11	Co-workers are intrigued with the opportunities that he identifies.	Less reliable	Reliable	Strong	
12	He provides leadership in his area.	Less reliable	Reliable	Strong	
13	He believes that ambiguity opens possibilities.	Less reliable	Reliable	Strong	
14	He is committed to his success.	Less reliable	Reliable	Strong	
15	He is committed to his organization's success.	Less reliable	Reliable	Strong	
16	I believe that he works hard *and* regularly makes time for other important aspects of his life.	Less reliable	Reliable	Strong	
17	I believe that while work is important to him, he makes time for his family and for himself.	Less reliable	Reliable	Strong	

	Attributes	A 3rd-Tier Attribute	A 2nd-Tier Attribute	A 1st-Tier Attribute	✓
18	He is aligned with his organization's values and vision.	Less reliable	Reliable	Strong	
19	It is important to him that he is aligned with his organization's values and vision.	Less reliable	Reliable	Strong	
20	His organization values what he does.	Less reliable	Reliable	Strong	
21	He enjoys working as part of a great team.	Less reliable	Reliable	Strong	
22	He does not need to lead every team that he is on.	Less reliable	Reliable	Strong	
23	People seek out his thinking on their work.	Less reliable	Reliable	Strong	
24	He represents the company well, both internally and externally.	Less reliable	Reliable	Strong	
25	He is respected by his peers and by senior management.	Less reliable	Reliable	Strong	
26	He projects his commitment to the success of our venture.	Less reliable	Reliable	Strong	

	Attributes	A 3rd-Tier Attribute	A 2nd-Tier Attribute	A 1st-Tier Attribute	✓
27	He functions well as a member of a team.	Less reliable	Reliable	Strong	
28	He puts people at ease.	Less reliable	Reliable	Strong	
29	He is trusted.	Less reliable	Reliable	Strong	
30	People like to work with him; they seek him out.	Less reliable	Reliable	Strong	
31	He is willing to take risks, to push the existing methods to make improvements.	Less reliable	Reliable	Strong	
32	He can succeed anywhere in the organization.	Less reliable	Reliable	Strong	
33	He displays dedication, confidence, a passion for his job, and a sense of urgency.	Less reliable	Reliable	Strong	
34	He is flexible when obstacles surface.	Less reliable	Reliable	Strong	
35	He is a creative thinker.	Less reliable	Reliable	Strong	
36	He is critical thinker.	Less reliable	Reliable	Strong	
37	He is good at helping others succeed.	Less reliable	Reliable	Strong	

	Attributes	A 3rd-Tier Attribute	A 2nd-Tier Attribute	A 1st-Tier Attribute	✓
38	When faced with a problem, he can make decisions.	Less reliable	Reliable	Strong	
39	He makes decisions and can enforce them when needed.	Less reliable	Reliable	Strong	
40	He will decide and act on less than complete information.	Less reliable	Reliable	Strong	
41	He knows what is right and wrong when faced with a dilemma.	Less reliable	Reliable	Strong	
42	He makes decisions based on clear criteria.	Less reliable	Reliable	Strong	
43	He responds well in a crisis.	Less reliable	Reliable	Strong	
44	He has the expertise needed for his role.	Less reliable	Reliable	Strong	
45	He seeks out the expertise of others.	Less reliable	Reliable	Strong	
46	He is happy to include the thinking of others whose expertise is greater than his.	Less reliable	Reliable	Strong	
47	Others follow his lead.	Less reliable	Reliable	Strong	

	Attributes	A 3rd-Tier Attribute	A 2nd-Tier Attribute	A 1st-Tier Attribute	✓
48	He knows how to do his job.	Less reliable	Reliable	Strong	
49	He knows when he needs help and gets it.	Less reliable	Reliable	Strong	
50	He performs his defined role very well.	Less reliable	Reliable	Strong	
51	He creates value for his team, for his department, for his organization or for his profession.	Less reliable	Reliable	Strong	
52	He manages people well.	Less reliable	Reliable	Strong	
53	He is good at developing the people on his team.	Less reliable	Reliable	Strong	
54	He is seen as someone who helps others succeed.	Less reliable	Reliable	Strong	
55	He can make his ideas operational.	Less reliable	Reliable	Strong	
56	He finds that others value what he does.	Less reliable	Reliable	Strong	
57	He prefers work that requires him to learn new skills and/or ideas.	Less reliable	Reliable	Strong	
58	He likes challenges.	Less reliable	Reliable	Strong	

	Attributes	A 3rd-Tier Attribute	A 2nd-Tier Attribute	A 1st-Tier Attribute	✓
59	He prefers to work on new tasks.	Less reliable	Reliable	Strong	
60	He relishes taking on a challenge that requires him to learn new skills. Number of marks in each column should equal 20	Less reliable 20	Reliable 20	Strong 20	

Corporate MVPs, Copyright 2004

Please return this completed form to the person you rated.

丮

Detailed Job and Person Description

Position Summary, Senior Vice President, Human Resources

Position Summary

The Senior Vice President of Human Resources for Company X will operate as a key member of the top management team reporting to and working closely with the President and Chief Executive Officer. He/she will partner with the executive team to enhance the Company's position as a leader in the industry. The Senior Vice President of Human Resources will plan and implement the human capital strategy for the company, focusing on organizational and talent trends, compensation and benefit strategies, morale, employee relations and issues that relate to the company's future development. He/she will function as a close confidant to the senior management team, providing expert advice on technical human resources issues. He/she will be responsible for enhancing and developing the talent of the Company's high-potential employees. At the same time, this person needs to have a bottom-line orientation, focusing on business strategy, budgeting, operating profits and effective cost management.

Relationships

Reports to:	President and Chief Executive Officer
Key Relationships:	(Lists out the key peers that the person will have to work with)
Other Key Relationships:	Outside consultants Human Resource Committee of the Board
Direct Reports:	Five direct reports

Major Responsibilities and Expected Results

- Function as the top talent and organizational strategist, as well as a key advisor to senior management on all human capital issues.

- Enable the organization to achieve growth goals by architecting innovative ways to attract, motivate and retain talent.

- Work with senior management to ensure that the values, strategy, structure, skills, systems and processes of the organization are aligned for success.

- Align the human resources function and effort with the business strategy and economic model of the company.

- Provide thorough leadership and initiatives around people and organizational issues so that the company benefits from and capitalizes on its organizational/people strengths.

- Ensure that the necessary human resources infrastructure is in place to institutionalize first-rate human resources practices. Hire, train and manage direct reports within the human resources department to ensure that objectives are achieved, including financial objectives. Provide guidance to both direct and indirect reports as needed.

- Institute programs and initiatives that enhance the organization's culture.
- Personally lead executive development-related programs, such as
  - functioning as a confidential advisor on sensitive personnel matters
  - coaching and team building
  - facilitating change and advancing change management practices
  - ensuring that training and development programs are developed that link to the goals and objectives of the organization
  - facilitating succession planning and related developmental activities
  - consulting with senior management in departments on employee development and performance management issues
- Ensure that the organization's compensation and benefits are evaluated, rationalized, optimized and clearly communicated.
- Ensure adherence to all legal requirements.
- Operate within the budget of $------------.

Key Competencies and Previous Experience

- A track record of achieving significant organizational and cultural change.
- A strong leader with good analytical skills, a serious human resources perspective, as well as excellent listening and influence skills. Someone to be taken seriously, but fun to be around.
- Able to establish a vision for, and implement, a world-class human resources function.
- State-of-the-art, comprehensive knowledge of the human resource processes with generalist experience. Exposure to

all core functions within the discipline. Good grounding in the areas of organizational development and compensation and benefits.

- A proven track record of working as a business partner with line managers in the design and implementation of value-added, customer-driven human resources programs and services. This experience includes success as an advisor, counselor and confidant to operating executives. Should be comfortable both providing support for and, as appropriate, challenging the thinking of senior executives.
- A personally credible and trustworthy leader who uses leadership and vision to motivate members to achieve goals.
- A background in financial services is preferred.
- An excellent fit with the company management team, which requires an intellectually curious, results-oriented, creative, even-tempered and participative-natured person.

The Ideal Person

- A commitment to the company's mission and purpose. An individual devoted to making the company a career destination for the truly talented.
- An energetic, results-driven and service-oriented executive who has a solid grasp of financial and corporate goals and the role the human resources function can play in achieving corporate objectives, managing costs and achieving change.
- A mature, confident individual who can act as a trusted advisor, confidant and representative of senior management. A person of character with a reputation for integrity.
- A superior strategist/businessperson with a passion for talent, leadership, organization development and corporate culture.

- A proactive professional with effective consultative skills, able to forge and maintain close relationships.

- A proven leader with excellent persuasion and negotiation skills who has the ability to be successful in an open, participative environment.

- Outstanding strategic-planning and problem-solving capabilities; someone who can approach issues from a strategic and business perspective and develop solutions centered for people and talent.

Index